THE SOCIETY OF
CLASSICAL POETS

JOURNAL VII

Mantyk · Phillips · Anderson · Grein

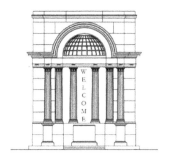

RhetAskew Publishing

United States of America

Editors
Evan Mantyk, Connie Phillips,
C.B. Anderson, Dusty Grein

Layout by Dusty Grein
Journal Art Editor: Daniel Magdalen
All contemporary artwork used
with permission of the artist.

Cover art: Detail of *Weight of Sacrifice* by Sabin Howard
"The Society of Classical Poets Edifice"
on cover and title page by Michael Curtis

Inquiries and Membership
submissions@classicalpoets.org

*RhetAskew Publishing is a division of Rhetoric Askew, LLC. All intellectual
property rights are held by The Society of Classical Poets, RhetAskew Publishing,
and/or the poets and artists whose work is featured within.*

ISBN-13: 978-1-949398-11-3
ISBN-10: 1-949398-11-0

Contents

INTRODUCTION

The cover of this Journal depicts the bronze relief, *The Weight of Sacrifice*, by sculptor Sabin Howard, which is part of the planned National World War I Memorial set for Pershing Square in Washington, D.C. It will be the World War I memorial that the American capital has long been missing. Though the relief is not yet built (the cover image is of a detail of a model), it has been approved by the U.S. Congress. This work, which will stand 65 feet long and 11 feet high when complete, is a major victory for classical arts. Rather than creating a weird, post-modern monument that ignores the human form and attempts to subvert the traditional perspective, Mr. Howard has harnessed the power and beauty of tradition to plan a work that inspires and ennobles the spirit. This is precisely what we aim to do at The Society of Classical Poets.

I met Mr. Howard about seven years ago in his Bronx art studio. I was interviewing him for an article in *The Epoch Times*. Walking in and viewing so many incredible figures sculpted in the images of gods and with a clear and unsoiled vision of beauty was truly astounding; I felt like the world was waking up to what art could be. Not long after, the Society's first Journal, published in 2013, included a photo of an Apollo sculpture by Mr. Howard and a sonnet in its praise. I could tell that Mr. Howard, whom I was quite possibly the first to interview and take seriously as a journalist at the time, was on his way up. Now he is being interviewed by Fox News, *The Wall Street Journal*, *The Weekly Standard*, *The New Yorker* (whose poetry I cannot vouch for), and many other major media outlets.

I see in the poets of The Society of Classical Poets, and those artists who have lent their artwork to this *Journal*, the same incredible but relatively ignored potential and the same appreciation for discipline, beauty, and tradition that I saw in Mr. Howard's Bronx studio seven years ago. You—the poets, writers, and appreciators of the Society—are on your way up.

But the way up is not easy. The development and growth of the Society has not been easy and, for this reason, I will offer some words of advice to readers as well. Communism is not merely a political ideology or definition in a Global History textbook. It is a real and living bane to humanity and most commonly goes under the name of socialism today, but it is also found under liberalism, progressivism, and even open-mindedness, inclusivity, or "don't be such a fascist"-ism. For frequent readers, it may sound as if I am preaching to the choir (after all, we already have a chapter called "Exposing Communism"). But to understand how deeply important this perspective is, we can go no further than the topic of this introduction: the cover art. You may look around at other poetry journals and individual poets' books, and it is very unlikely that you will see any serious ones depicting war or combat on the cover. The snide observer might spit from his mouth, "I thought it said the Society of Classical Militarists," and the cooler, more academic sort may cleverly opine that poetry should bring peace, harmony, and an end to man's struggles against his fellow man. This latter perspective may seem reasonable, but it is actually not for two reasons:

First, it completely ignores history. The history of war poetry is long, though it peters out in the last century. Most recent are the War Poets of World War I and the anachronistic General George Patton. These poets are mere vestiges as communism and its agenda rose at this time. If we travel back to the Renaissance, though, the story changes and war is featured prominently in Shakespeare's *Hamlet, Julius Caesar, Henry V,* and many other works (most of these works being poetic for their iambic pentameter and occasional rhyming). Going further back, we are fully into the splendid tradition of medieval romantic poetry, involving knights and inevitably wars, as found in the *La Chanson de Roland (The Song of Roland)*, Arthurian literature, Chaucer's *Canterbury Tales, El Cantar de Mio Cid (The Poem of The Cid)*, and many others. Further still, and we are into antiquity with Homer's *Iliad* and *Odyssey* and Virgil's *Aeneid*. Ignoring such history may seem like no big deal in the cushy seat of the present, but even that willingness to forget is the work of communism, which devalues history and works toward a deceptive utopia of the future. Without history, we are nothing.

War has always been a defining feature of humanity, and out of it arise heroes, honor, valor, loyalty, justice, chivalry, and so on. These are absolutely worth celebrating in sculptures, poetry, or any art form.

Second, the glorification of peace and the demonization of war, though they are nothing new in the course of history, have reached extreme and irrational extents in the public consciousness. This development is not a natural phenomenon, but the direct result of the work of communists during the Cold War years using peace as a means of stalling and destabilizing an enemy so that the Soviet Union had enough time to build and develop a nuclear arsenal.

The Epoch Times commentary *How the Specter of Communism Is Ruling Our World* states:

> *Having suffered huge losses in the war, the Soviet Union aggressively promoted world peace as a stratagem to stave off pressure from the West. The World Peace Council was directly controlled by the Soviet Peace Commission, an organization affiliated with the Soviet Communist Party. It ran a worldwide narrative proclaiming the Soviet Union to be a peace-loving country and condemning the United States as a hegemonic warmonger...*
>
> *According to the testimony of Stanislav Lunev, a former officer of the Soviet GRU (military intelligence) who defected from Russia to the United States in 1992, the amount of money the Soviet Union spent on antiwar propaganda in Western countries was double its military and economic support to North Vietnam. He said that "the GRU and KGB financed almost all antiwar movements and groups in the United States and other countries."*

The details of the infiltration into democratic societies go on and on. The relatively benign-seeming peace marches and hippie culture of the 1960s and 1970s were thus put on steroids by Soviet money and influence. The Soviet Union, and those duped communists who salivated over its rise, succeeded in creating an aura of enlightened intellectualism around peace and an intense aversion for the savagery of war that were out of touch with reality. This distorted perspective is the one that mainstream culture has adopted.

3

I recommend that everyone read the entire *Epoch Times* commentary series mentioned above. It can be accessed online for free (TheEpochTimes.com). It is translated from the writings of Chinese scholars living in the West, and though the language is not particularly elegant, its points are truly enlightening and perspective-shattering.

It is easy in our day-to-day interactions to lose sight of who the enemy is and who the good guys are. Communism and socialism, and their modernist aesthetic, are the real enemy of every man, woman, and child on Earth. Indeed, the cover art can be viewed not as a struggle of man against man, but of the human spirit against the force of communism that was rising in the world at the time. Communism, among the Allied Powers, would topple the Russian czar near the end of the war, leading to the rise of the Bolsheviks and then Soviets. Among the Central Powers, communist tendencies would topple the German kaiser and lead to the rise of the National Socialists—the Nazis (whose Darwin inspired eugenics led to such infamous atrocities).

Finally, then, it is up to us to carry on and win the battle. Not by throwing barbs at each other, but by working together with an appreciation for tradition and for excellence and with a sense of revived chivalry—what the anonymous 14th-century *Sir Gawain* poet called fellowship, generosity, piety, cleanness, and courtesy (*felaschyp, fraunchyse, pite, clannes, cortaysye*). We must continue writing classical poetry and allowing it to inform whatever endeavors have been laid before us by hands greater than our own.

—Evan Mantyk, Society President

I. BEAUTY

Lake Solitude by Mark Keathley, 54 x 48 in., oil on canvas, 2008.

Common Language

by Mike Ruskovich

I hear the music of the artist's brush
Bruise with color the canvas' white,
Feel the composer's fingers rush
Across the keyboard into night
To lodge clear notes in the blackest sky,
Stars for some poor poet to ponder,
For some sculptor to absorb and sigh
While letting the free muse wander.

I taste the red of the ancient rose
Hanging framed upon the wall
And smell the thought the thinker knows
On sojourns through bright leaves that fall
On landscapes painted long ago,
From symphonies that shake the trees,
Oils that chill the scene with snow,
And portraits of Jesus on Mary's knees.

The masters rarely missed the mark;
Perfection was their recompense,
A light that pierced the primal dark
And bathed the soul and every sense
With what would fly beyond their hands
To fill the eyes and ears and hearts
Of distant souls in foreign lands
Who speak the language of the arts.

Heritage

by C. David Hay

Behold the cloud-graced monoliths
That stretch against the sky
Into the boundless sanctity
Where wind-swift eagles fly.

Primal valleys bloom to life
As tumbling waters sing,
Resurrected from the heights
Where ancient glaciers cling.

Time is without measure
In a world no one can claim;
Blessèd be the wilderness—
For freedom is its name.

Will we ever understand,
These are places where
Mortal hands cannot improve
The beauty God put there.

To Nicholas Wilton

traditional sacred polyphonist of England

by Joseph Charles MacKenzie

Wilton! Could music make the dead to rise,
Spare life its toil, move wills from sloth,
Bind happy lovers in their troth,
Or lift a heart to soar upon the skies,

Rather would I your holy strains to hear,
That breathe of the eternal life
And free the spirit of its strife,
As if to sanctify the human ear.

Our times find balance in your measured tones
That raise the sweetness of your lays
To heights of consecrated praise
Resounding in the far celestial zones!

Through you the souls of Tallis and of Byrd
Respire the chaste sobriety
Of England's antique piety
In youthful melodies before unheard.

May you, who snatched from Orpheus his lyre,
To play it at Our Lady's feet,
Forever make man's heart to beat
With love of Him who fuels your music's fire!

Benedictum Nomen Mariæ

by Joseph Charles MacKenzie

Her name is like the rain-perfumèd air
Of summer on a lost and winsome day:
I breathe it and am free of every care,
I say it and want nothing more to say.

Her name is laden like the honeycomb
Whose sweetness penetrates the yielding depth
Of all my soul, and, like the thought of home,
To think on her consoles and eases breath.

Her intercessions lift the weight of sin,
And just as wax doth melt before the flame,
Or as a frown dissolves into a grin,
All darkness flees before her holy name.

Maria! Be thy name at life's eclipse
The final sound that leaves my dying lips.

The Mellow Season

by Carole Mertz

Ah, now comes the mellow season,
Marks its time with jackdaws' caws.
Autumn with its rusty reason
Offers forth its season's laws.

Now no more the pretty laces,
Florals found along the way.
Brackish forms in darker traces,
Longer shadows, shorter day.

Autumn wears its gown of orange
Trampling out the summer's green.
Skunks and jays and squirrels forage,
Welcome soon a wintry scene.

Listening to the Lark

on Ralph Vaughan Williams' The Lark Ascending,
a romance for violin and orchestra inspired by
George Meredith's poem of the same title

by Daniel Magdalen

Past years of smoke and pain, a tune in ether flows
Untouched, while spreading forth from inspiration's spring:
Swift crystal tones unite in winding flight to bring
The lark to life, from words in which its song once rose.

A sylvan scene of yore is summoned through a string,
Far, lost to time, yet to our feeling's pulse so near—
The rushing wings of sound, the breathless voice we hear
Reflect a life that's there no more to rise and sing...

Perceptions come to deepen, further as we peer
Through olden times' clear lens of peacefulness and care
For life's pure colors few now know and fewer share,
Thus, less can these live on with each new clouded year.

A wordless poem crystallizes in the air,
Addressing all who pause to listen and can gaze
Above the ceaseless to and fro of earthbound days;
For to our fleeting focus, nothing's pictured there.

The tuneful echoes brighten, piercing through the haze
Of self-absorption, as a waking call to keep
Alive each creature's destined voice... The lark may leap
Then toward tomorrow, further trails of song to blaze.

The Birdman of Gdansk

by Leo Yankevich

When cathedral bells toll through the morning
and sunlight touches steeples with its glare,
and arrows on the town hall clock stop turning,
you will find him on the market square,
sweeping leaves in shadows of despair.
And in that instant you will cease your yearning.
Hunchbacked, with a chuckle he will share
the secrets of his heart, and give a warning
to city doves assembling at his feet,
to sparrows quarreling on Neptune's head.
He'll lower his tobacco chin to meet
their eyes and whisper what Saint Francis said.
He'll toss crumbs with his withered sailor's hand.
And when he looks up, you will understand.

Let There Be Light

by Kim Cherub

"Cherubim and Seraphim, assemble and salute!
Behold your Lord's creation; let every tongue fall mute."
Thus Michael spoke for all, enthralled, dazed by the stars' bright rays:
"Oh who among us—dazzled, awed—dare sing the Maker's praise?"

But never fear, the Lord Himself has made fine instruments
And tuned them with precision for man's future testaments.
As eagles are endowed with wings to wheel and soar and climb,
True poets will be given gifts: pure rhythm, reason, rhyme.

But let such gifts be guarded from imposters soon to come;
Be careful this fine banquet does not end up one stale crumb.
For, as devils infiltrate the church and lead its flocks astray,
So too with sheepish poets: evil wolves will have their way.

And yet a stalwart remnant will not desert the Lord;
His paradise awaits them—yea, behold the covering sword!
The wise will always praise Him; the foolish, to their doom,
Will follow falsest "prophets" into the formless gloom.

True poets, tune your meter! True poets of the lyre,
Make your voices heard above the gibberings from the mire!
For soon the Day of Judgment comes; the Marriage Feast awaits;
But talents squandered fund the tolls exacted at hell's gates.

It…

by Daniel Leach

It plays upon the glowing, sunset boughs,
When shadows have enveloped all below,
And distant, other-worldly thoughts arouse
A passion in the poet's soul to go
Beyond the earth, beyond the dark'ning sky,
Where only unembodied spirits fly.

It beckons coyly in that certain look
The woodland flower wears in the morning light,
Half-hidden in the shadows, by a brook
Which murmurs gently, as if to invite
The mind in endless beauties to immerse,
Unfolding in its little universe.

It guides by unseen force the flock of birds
That swirls and soars upon the twilight air,
And all that lives and breathes, as if by words
Unspoken, though however unaware,
Yet dance as its mysterious music sways
And with our noblest thoughts of freedom, plays.

And then, it sometimes visits in a form
That haunts like some gigantic destiny;
The dark and threatening beauty of a storm
Whose coming flash of jagged light we see,
Yet feel, as all around the thunder rolls,
A primal freedom stirring in our souls.

But most, I see it in another's eyes,
That sparkle when a thought is born within,
Or fill with tears when holy passions rise
That speak of what could be, or could have been;
And I am in the presence of a force
That is all other earthly Beauty's source.

Revelation by Herman Smorenburg, 37.4 x 56.7 in., oil on wood, 2004.

The Snowflake

by Daniel Leach

The brooding mists of my thoughts haunt the morn,
And heavily upon the meadows lie,
Until, on faintly whispering winds, they're borne
Aloft, into the brightening morning sky,
And there, as if by magic, high above
The dreaming earth, dance with the rays of sun,
And are transformed by breath of Heaven's love
To infinitely lovely forms, each one
A miracle that never was before!
And like angels rejoicing in new birth,
In dazzling beauty for a moment soar
Above the clouds, then gently fall to earth;
They're mine no more than is the morning dew,
And so I leave them on the page for you.

Poems Unwritten

by Daniel Leach

Sometimes, when the light and the mists of the day
  Settle holy and soft on the edge of the night,
When the sights and the sounds of the world melt away,
  And the vision that lives in the soul takes flight,
    That feeling comes on I felt since I was young,
      Of poems unwritten and songs unsung.

Like a shadow that flits across the moonbeams
  Thrills the soul all the more for its dark mystery,
Or the memory in daytime of last night's dreams,
  Like another world under the surface we see,
    Like that thought that lives on the tip of the tongue,
      Are those poems unwritten and songs unsung.

In the gaze of the lover who grasps for a word
  To embody the feeling that's shared in the eyes,
Or forgotten strains of a song long unheard
  Whose sad memory deep in the heart still lies,
    Like all the new thoughts that ever have sprung,
      Are those poems unwritten and songs unsung.

It's there in the child as he sees the sublime
  In the greatness and beauty of life unfurled,
It lives in the instant, but outside of time,
  And comforts the dying as they leave this world;
    It sleeps in all souls though the lyre be unstrung,
      Those poems unwritten and songs unsung.

In the Deep of the Night

by Daniel Leach

In the deep of the night do my restless thoughts roam
    To the moon-flooded fields of the sky,
And they search for a pure and ethereal home,
    Where emotions and thoughts never die.

Where the mountains and valleys of silvery cloud
    Are eternally calling to me,
And the star-written secrets their vapors enshroud
    Stretch beyond, like an infinite sea!

Where the souls of the dead and the millions unborn,
    All around me, suffused in soft light,
Purest colors, like jewels, my pathway adorn,
    To my earth-weighted vision give sight.

And that light is a love that on earth we but guess
    In our purest and loveliest dreams,
And with some higher passion those spirits caress,
    Upward-drawing the soul with their beams.

For I know that among them are those I did love,
    When together we walked o'er the earth,
Like a voice on the wind from the regions above,
    Call me back to the place of my birth.

Moonlight Secret by Herman Smorenburg, 30.7 x 55.1 in., oil on wood, 2007.

To Old Friends

by Joshua Philipp

Around the bonfire, we were brothers who sang
Of joys that are gone, and the flame turned to ash
And blew on the wind to where endless stars hang
In search of past embers that flicker and flash.

How strange is the feeling of mortal life's dance
The wheel of all souls and of gratitude's debt.
How friendship's long ties can our own lives enhance
With meaning from travelers we once had met.

Yet far and beyond me, my friends have outrun.
Alone now I visit that circle of old
Where coals of my memory, lit by the sun
That fades like our dreams in the creeping of cold.

Yet maybe we'll meet in the end, reignite;
Again we'll be brothers and sing in delight.

Armed with Imagination

by Randal A. Burd, Jr.

Imagination armed this youthful knight—
a plywood shield and sword of sapling wood
created echoes in the neighborhood
of backyard battles fought in fading light.

Envision how we must have been a sight
to see—a panorama understood
by only we who fought each chance we could
while lacking rhyme or reason for a fight.

The best of memories those days remain:
each noble quest and faux chivalric deed.
Forever will they be accompanied
with yearning for just one last grand campaign.

Artisans & Fools

by Randal A. Burd, Jr.

The sparks of protest fly as hammer pounds
To make a stubborn ingot sharper steel.
In pummeling, perfection will reveal
Its shifting shape with banging clanging sounds.
This repetition lasts for several rounds;
As smithy molds, the metal does appeal
For mercy from relentless hammer's zeal;
The artisan, in answer, only frowns.

When flames are duly doused and metal cools,
The finished product's polish is applied;
And, only then, the maker will decide
If labor's love was worthy of his tools.
Its quality has thus identified
The difference in artisans and fools.

Blue Spacious Skies

a rondeau

by Randal A. Burd, Jr.

Blue spacious skies meet greener pastures' hue,
Where sleepy woodland creatures rendezvous.
The fragrances of lilac and of fir
Are pungent in the air and would confer
A feeling of tranquility on you.

Your present rather dismal point of view
Is neither flexible nor even true.
You bring the rain; your outlook does defer
Blue spacious skies.

So open wide the door; let sunshine through.
Find shooting stars at night with someone new.
Our lives go by in such a hasty blur.
You'll see things better than they ever were.
And cloudy days might suddenly incur
Blue spacious skies.

A Rounded Stone

by Benjamin Daniel Lukey

He pressed a rounded stone into my hand.
He said, "Take care of this," and turned away
To tend to things we needed for our trip:
The boats, the lines, the paddles, and the rest.

The stone was not like those about my feet.
I wondered at the stone, but not for long.
I put it in my pocket and forgot.

The Huzzah winds along a valley floor
Between thick stands of trees and rocky bluffs.
Its water is a marvel to behold,
Like crystal ichor flowing in God's veins.
I thought of all these things, and not the stone,
But in my pocket it was safe and sound.

And that was well, for when we came ashore
My uncle asked me for the rounded stone.
He placed it on the bank beside its twin.

"As easy as it was for you," he said,
"To bring this back to where I picked it up,
So light you sit within your Maker's hand.
The stone was not aware you carried it,
And sometimes we are just the same. But He
Is wise, and kind, and big and strong enough
To bring you safely to your journey's end.
We're going where we came from." So he said.

I miss him, but I know we'll meet again.

I Journey On

a villanelle

by James A. Tweedie

The sun descends into the silent sea.
As shadows lengthen in the fading light
I journey on to seek what yet may be.

As death from life yearns to be free,
And grief seeks comfort in the night,
The sun descends into the silent sea.

And as the past with all its misery
Sets with the sun and disappears from sight,
I journey on to seek what yet may be.

And as for love there is no guarantee.
For whether one is in the wrong or right,
The sun descends into the silent sea.

From pain and suffering no one can flee.
And so, amidst the brokenness and blight,
I journey on to seek what yet may be.

Yet hidden in this pain is harmony.
Within my heart its whispered dream burns bright.
The sun descends into the silent sea;
I journey on to seek what yet may be.

The Fairies Danced

by James A. Tweedie

The fairies danced and shone like diamonds on
   The lake below. My pole across my knees;
   My creel on my lap; the sun and trees
   Stood still; the mountain breeze had passed and gone.
I sat on granite, smooth and cool, and chose
   A fly (a Royal Coachman) which I tied
   On tightly to my line. Alone, I sighed,
   And smiled and paused and idly rubbed my nose.
I thought I was alone, but blur of white,
   Not seen, but sensed, alighted on my arm.
   A butterfly! A gentle, weightless kiss
   And it was gone. A gift of love so right
   And innocent. My heart felt strangely warm.
   The Realm of God must surely be like this.

The Squires of Roland by Ferdinand Becker, watercolor painting,
1876, exhibited at The Landesmuseum Mainz.

Of Roland and of Kings

by James A. Tweedie

I sing of Arthur and Excalibur,
The Table Round and fealty professed
By knights devoted to a noble quest
For what was right and good, and pure.

I sing of Percival and Bedivere;
Of Tristan, Kay, Gareth, and Adragain;
Of Galahad, Gaheris, and Gawain;
Of Lancelot Du Lac… and Guinevere.

I sing of Merlin, and the sordid plot
Of Mordred's treachery, and vows betrayed;
Of Holy Grail and promises unmade.
I sing of chivalry and Camelot.

I sing of Roland and of Durendal,
And those who fought and fell at Roncevaux
Defending France against a Muslim foe
Who sought to hold all Christendom in thrall.

I sing of Oliver and knightly pride,
Of noble warriors on the field slain,
Of truant Oliphant, and Charlemagne
Who wept when he discovered all had died.

I sing of minstrels and of Taillefer
Who sang of Roland as the battle raged
At Hastings and, with sword in hand, engaged
The foe and died, a gallant *ioglere*.

ioglere: minstrel

I sing of kings and knights, of serfs and vassals.
Regal queens and outlaw paladins;
Of jousts, and tournaments, and talismans;
Of troubadours and crenellated castles.

I sing of battles won and kingdoms lost.
I sing of Stirling Bridge and Agincourt;
Of Bannockburn, Nicopolis, and Tours;
Each one a savage, feudal holocaust.

I sing of glory, shame, and sacrifice.
I sing of power gained by force of might
And freedom wrested back from evil's blight.
And those who bore the cost and paid the price.

I sing of ages long since passed away,
Of martyr, hero, saint, and vagabond,
Who each survived their own slough of despond
To teach us and inspire us today.

I sing of history and what has been,
And though the past shines like a distant star
It nonetheless is part of who we are;
Our heritage of glory and chagrin.

I sing of ancient, Medieval things
To help ensure their memory survives.
Such memories illuminate our lives,
And so, I sing of Roland and of kings.

Ancient Melodies

by Ercules Edibwa, BDW*

No longer are they heard, the ancient melodies
of Greece, so beautiful and lovely to the ear.
One now can only imagine their mellow ease
played o'er the centuries, so far are they from here.
Like waters from th' Aegean Sea, they lap upon
the rocky shores of sandy, sunlit yesteryear
and splash in waves of luscious foam in rosy dawn.
That music draws us back to simpler times and ways,
but they, like those of then, are all forever gone;
and yet we long for them—those wonderful, sweet lays,
those haunting and inviting sounds, those bellowings
beyond our world, our understanding, and our praise.

* Bruce Dale Wise (aka BDW) is a poet living in Texas who often writes under anagrammatic heteronyms.

A Summer's Day

by Joe Tessitore

Blue skies at sunrise,
   The dawn of the day;
Clouds in the heavens
   That drift where they may;
Showers of flowers
   Aswirl on the breeze;
Petals that settle
   Wherever they please;
Honey bees hover
   Alighting upon
Buds that unfurl
   With the grace of the swan;
Daisies that sway
   In the gentle moonlight;
Crickets in thickets,
   The chorus of night.

The Dance of Life

by Joe Tessitore

Performance of unending grace,
the dance of life proceeds apace
to rhythms played throughout the years,
transcendent music of the spheres;
exquisite movements intertwine,
their choreography divine,
a work in progress, parts for all,
the never-ending curtain call.

My New Year's Resolution

by Joe Tessitore

I touch the paper with my pen
and so it comes alive again,
to speak with those I'll never see—
what message will it send from me?

Will I stand firm; will I not bend
and battle till the bitter end,
determined to annihilate
with poisoned words that spring from hate?

Or will I, like a little boy,
write simple words of peace and joy,
whose childlike innocence and charm
may bring a smile and might disarm?

I look within, whence I must start,
to see what lives inside my heart.

The Prodigal

by Joe Tessitore

As I return, late in the day,
crushed by a debt I can't repay,
aware of what I've put you through,
I dare not raise my eyes to you.

Then this—too much to understand—
you turn to me and take my hand!
I struggle for a word to say,
but you just brush my tears away.

Boldly did I dare to wander.
Coldly did I choose to squander
all that you could e'er impart—
the gift of your most loving heart.

My arrogance led me astray.
Your mercy called me home to stay.

Dryads' Winter Lament

by Wandi Zhu

As autumn breezes blow away
The warmth of summer's sun,
Then shortened is the light of day
When we had danced as one.

The prelude to the winter snow
Is sung by icy rain,
The rosiness of dawn's soft glow
Usurped by cloudy stains.

The bitter winds strip off the trees
Their red and golden leaves.
Our tears met by the North wind freeze.
Trees barren, bleak, we grieve.

The winter days we pass in dreams
Of fragrances of spring,
Of murmurs of the waking stream
And songs the birds will sing.

Farewell, farewell, sweet summer days
That blessed us with birdsong,
Adieu, bright flames of autumn's blaze,
Pray winter won't be long.

The Bluebonnet Sonnet

by Fr. Richard Libby

When spring arrives, the wildflow'rs start to grow
In woods and fields, and by the country lanes.
In reds and yellows, see the vernal show,
Inaugurated by the winter rains!

But in the state of Texas, we can say
That springtime has a quite distinctive hue;
The state's official flower has its day,
And crowns the grassy green with royal blue.

The bluebonnets can be seen far and wide
Beside each farm road, interstate, and route.
For passersby, the bluebonnets provide
A charming roadside floral photo shoot.

The springtime brings us quite a lovely view
In Texas, where both skies and flow'rs are blue.

Battle

Pigeon Cove, Massachusetts, 1948

by Florence Adams Clark

Above, the sky, remote and pure,
Below, the earth, steadfast and sure.
Between the two, the surging sea,
Fighting both for mastery.

Blue swell of wave, foam flung high,
White flash of challenge to proud sky,
The surge, the crash, the sounding roar
Of wind-swept wave on earth's stone door.

How Would We Like Our Existence To Be?

by Alessio Zanelli

Meaningful, interesting, active and strong.
  Simply, not counting the days, as if stray,
    dreary, unworthy, but making them count,
serve, be remembered and blest all along.
  Challenges ought to be faced on the way,
    obstacles scattered for us to surmount.

We would meander through deserts at length,
  probe the abysses of oceans and peaks,
    capture the glitter of stars from the sky.
That would require every bit of our strength,
  surely the best of our skills and mystiques.
    Only such wonders could surfeit our eye.

The Concert

July 17, 2016

by Lynn Michael Martin

We looked imploring to the starless sky;
we worlds and worlds of darkness, seeking light,
that we might momently forget our night;
for that strange hope we held, we knew not why.
And then it came, and then our tiring eye
it overwhelmed in one bright burst of white—
one moment it eclipsed all other light,
and passed again, and left an empty sky.
And oh! for ages our best fires might burn;
for ages store in hope their dear-bought strength,
yet die unheeded, lost in one such sight!
Come, let us leave these meager things, and turn,
and where the true heart leads us; there, at length,
our tear-washed eyes may drink eternal light.

The Warrior's Song at Dusk

by Ramón Rodriguez, LC

At last, some time to catch my breath
—a rest, a respite in the fight—
How many times I parried death!
Bask now in this fast-fading light.
   Behold the whispering golden sea
   so wide—see it inside of me.

The day's end finds this carcass sore
This tender flesh all fresh with pain
Yet still alive, this battered corpse:
Life seeps throughout my very veins.
   Look up and see the star-specked sky
   so high—see it inside my mind.

The first few fireflies appear
to fill the air. Behind me lies
the carnage of a duel: I fear
it's me who lives, and me who dies.
   This tortuous trail, years from the start,
   is held, each mile, in my heart.

My Garden

by Adam Sedia

Lush, fresh-pruned verdure shades the cobbled path,
It bursts with rich-hued blossoms strewn about
Whence sweet aromas waft, blend, and enswathe,
And droops with luscious, nectar-swollen fruit.

But leaves spread greedily to hoard the light;
And tendrils curl to choke a rival stem.
And upstarts rise amid the blooms to fight,
Usurp their place, and wrest the life from them.

I am the gardener. This plot is mine.
My spade and hoe, my trowel and my shears
Uproot the weeds, prune back the errant vine
From fragile blooms and infant green fruit-spheres.

Without my steel-bladed autocracy
The fair and fruitful die in anarchy.

The Ocean Sea

by Adam Sedia

The waters that gleam turquoise here for miles
And shimmer with the tropics' blazing rays,
That lap the white-sand shores of verdant isles
As gently as the salty sea-breeze plays,

Are those that swell to lofty, frothing heights
Where screaming gales perturb the freezing brine,
And course beneath titanic sheets of ice,
And crush abyssal depths where no rays shine.

If they so fiercely rage a world away,
Cannot this blue serenity yield fast
To what their fleeting fancy flings its way—
A rushing tide, a roaring cyclone blast?

This peace lies at their mercy totally,
For they are but a single ocean sea.

The Setting and the Rising

by Adam Sedia

The lazy, golden disc that dimly glows
With gentle light and ponderously hangs
Amid a sky of crimson, mauve, and rose,
Descending calmly to the western flanks,

This very moment is to distant eyes
The youthful morning blaze, blindingly bright,
Ascending high and filling turquoise skies
With radiant streams of white-hot, diamond light.

The once-almighty light that ruled the day,
Now dwindles and flies steadily away
To leave our heavens cold and tenebrous.

What eyes awaken in what distant place
To greet the dying remnant's other face,
Beholding it as once it shone to us?

Jordan

by C.B. Anderson

Now, as I gaze across the river
To moorings on the other side,
An evening chill evokes a shiver
That ripples up and down my hide.

A star is rising in the east
To signal that the day is spent
And that a sinner should at least,
If only for a while, repent.

My errant feet might well get wet
Before I make the final crossing,
But better that than to beget
Eternities of bedtime tossing

And turning when the worldly lights
Go out. The Lord dispenses pardon
To those who use their last few nights
For making sure their hearts don't harden
Against preferred celestial flights.

But what am I, if not a fool
Who thought himself beyond retrieval?
My idle hands, the Devil's tool,
Should serve the Good and swat the Evil,
As practiced in the Master's school.

United They Fall

by C.B. Anderson

Exhausted armies cling to noble trees
along the margin of a meadow mown
two weeks ago. It's fifty-five degrees,

and summer's long campaign is at an end,
the bugles stilled, except when taps is blown—
for here and there a feckless golden horde,
a red brigade with nothing to defend,
and russet legions hoping brighter sun
will shine again upon their liege and lord.
As waning daylight fails the living crown,
dead soldiers break formation, one by one.

The law observed throughout this passing season
is uniform for woodland, farm, or town:
Each unsurrendered blade's an act of treason.

First published in Sonnetto Poesia
Vol. 9 nos. 2 & 3, Summer/Autumn 2010

Obituary

by C.B. Anderson

Late summer, when the bumblebees begin to die,
You'll see them clinging to the petals of a flower
For dear life—or at least it seems so to an eye
Untrained in entomology. They've had their hour,

Have likely reproduced authentic replicas,
And now are caught in the inanimate repose
They've earned by simply doing everything that was
Expected of them. No one living really knows

What colors stain the *Umwelt* of a bumblebee,
Or what compelling fragrance draws it to the nectar
Of which it drinks. The more complex reality
That human beings navigate—a private sector

Bound up with social threads—is plagued by states of mind
Which naturally arise inside a primate brain:
Perfunctory regret, and motive ill-defined;
The fear of losing hope, and existential pain.

Although at last you recognize how far you've fallen,
Belated clarity does nothing to forestall
What's bound to come. Too late it is to gather pollen,
But much too soon to die with flowers in the fall,
                    to hang your laurels on a wall,
                    to say you never lived at all.

Umwelt: the world as it is experienced by a particular organism

First published in Anglican Theological Review
Vol. 98 no. 3, Summer 2016

Island City: Auckland

by Jan Darling

I've grown to love this place of sea and noise
Where buildings have assumed a regal poise
As high they stab on sultry summer nights
Daring to dim the stars above their lights.
The neons flicker brazen into sky
And tinseled posters twinkle at each eye
Proclaiming that this city is alive
And recommending goods on which you'll thrive.
At midday pavements throb with office feet
In exodus to cafe bars to eat,
Their owners sipping coolness from the breeze
Which sidles through the streets from polished seas.

The beaches baking lazy to the east
Are spun with birds and shells and picnic feast
Quiescent waves creep gently to the shore
And drowsily retire to ocean floor.
An idle dinghy snoozes at its buoy
And dreams of leading warships in convoy;
And tiny sprat are entertaining thoughts
Of scuttling sharks at underwater sports;
Small birds untaught of Hitchcocks and Spiegels
Are planning to attack some legal eagles.
A feeble wind that scarcely quivers sails
In fancy lashes fearful schools of whales.

But beaches sprawling windswept to the west
Are bitterly symbolic in their quest
For souls to fill the coffers in their church
Where Poseidon reclaims from salty perch.
Here, winds in frenzy whip and splice each mound
And slouching crabs are snooping all around;
And even soft white seabirds lack a grace

As awkwardly they lumber wingèd space.
The jagged rocks stoop ugly from the tide
Where straggling seaweed strangles at each stride
The smold'ring sun the seaside reeds has baked
And smoothest rocks with vicious shells are caked.

These are the beaches of Time and Season
Demented waters of gnashing waves
Fired with reality, wild beyond reason
Conquering humans to be their slaves.

The Night

by Sathya Narayana

Wee hours, when crickets tune their eerie cords
and hoot the yawning owls at twinkling stars;
the night-maid roves seesaw, like a drunken bard,
besmeared with stripes of billion moonlight-scars!

A slithering thief along the parapet wall,
a snaking beau crossing the forlorn street,
a Robin chirping sweet on sandy knoll…
decrying all, she glides with nimble feet!

While slumbers world, in wonted joys and pain
of dreams, the sleepless Stygian Queen patrols
in peace, sans smiles or frowns, the earth and main,
till dawns the day-despot for glorious strolls.

But lo, unlike her Lord with blazing arms,
she's calm and rules the world with soothing balms!

Saint Agnes

by Fr. Bruce Wren

This evening of your festive day I pray
  Oh Agnes, little model of the pure,
  Oh girl with smiling eyes, and faith so sure:
They won for you the martyr's palm this day.
For neither threat nor coaxing in the fray
  Of that heroic battle was to lure
  You to a wedding couch or a life obscure
Within a stranger's arms... Better, away

Oh little lamb of white, to run and play
  Within the fields of heaven and the spring
    Of all that simple smiles has this age surprised
With innocence; and waken to the day
  That only eternity can see and sing,
    And flee into the arms of Jesus Christ.

In the Villa Comunale, Taormina

9 March 2018

by William Ruleman

The bushes shimmer, shedding dawn's dull shower:
Jasmine, trumpet vine conspire to join
The bougainvillea in fiery flower
Under Sun's still cloud-stained glowing coin.

I drink the scents in, greet the gurgling doves,
The bold birds singing in the cypresses:
The whole world seems to teem with little loves.
I strain to ken what every creature says.

With softened roar, the waves caress the shore.
Take your tone from us, I hear them say.
Quell your worldly quests, your lust for more.
Make all the music God can grant this day.

Pray that everyone on earth may find
This morning's mirthful mood and restful mind.

Mount Etna from Taormina by Thomas Cole, 48 x 32.5 in., oil on canvas, 1843, exhibited at Wadsworth Atheneum Museum of Art, Hartford, Connecticut.

The Archaeological Gardens at Giardini-Naxos

7 March 2018

by William Ruleman

The stones are overgrown with clover now,
Drowned by daisies, fresh cape sorrel too;
Orange or lemon globes gleam from each bough;
Mankind's Old's usurped by Nature's New.

To think such careful craft should come to this,
We muse while roaming at our modern ease.
God's art will conquer all our artifice
And leave the rubble to the brooding bees.

Autumn Trees

after Edger Allan Poe's "Bells"

by Evan Mantyk

See the passing forest trees—
Autumn trees!
How the garments of the year fall gently to their knees;
How they tumble, tumble, tumble
In the brilliant light of day
Midst the forest stream's soft mumble,
Cloudless sky that has no rumble
Under Heaven's mighty sway.
Shedding leaves, leaves, leaves,
How sublimely nature grieves!
What a lilting lamentation sung from lofty sylvan eaves:
When from trees' eaves leaves leave,
We perceive
Our own humbling in the crumbling of these trees.

A Life Well-Lived

a rondeau

by Caroline Bardwell

A life well-lived begins and ends
surrounded by the love of friends.
The air breathed in and out each lung
are signals that songs should be sung,
for life's a blessing God intends

A person who can make amends,
his honor and his name defends,
so that his hat can there be hung—
a life well-lived.

Who strives to save more than he spends
and if he can he freely lends,
who learns his lessons while he's young
and knows when he should bite his tongue;
with wisdom and with care he tends
a life well-lived.

Ode to Cole's "*The Titan's Goblet*"

by William Krusch

O Grand Enigma! Tower of Life! Thy lofty scene
   Is but the glimpse of that eternal mystery,
For in thy cup amidst the twilight's gloaming sheen,
   There whisper softly chords of immortality,
Resounding tones of universal harmony
   Which herald all the endless peace it brings to those
Who can decipher with thy signs eternity,
   And solve the ancient riddle of the blossomy rose.

Between thy verdurous, mossy banks, the Muse yet blows
   Its secrets 'cross the placid lake; that tranquil face
Reflects the images of buildings, gently throws
   Their marble visage o'er the waters with light grace—
These structures are the remnants of a bolder race,
   A race of gods who walked among the earth in times
When brilliant souls recalled that pillowed resting place
   From where the soul originates in distant climes.

O come, old noble thoughts! Now let me with soft rhymes
   Remember that high space where pure, transcendent thought
But forms the architecture of the universe, and primes
   The mind, so sorely yearning, for what is but sought
Within the dreamer's sleep—Truth. Yes—the Truth is brought
   Into the Light, and now the wisdom of all things
Is known through revelation—loose, mind! loose the knot
   Of all the hidden wisdom! End our sufferings!

Alas—the path is clouded still; our wanderings
   Are but a dreary march amidst the ceaseless toil
Of vain existence; O, Life! O'er the sea there sings
   The murmurs of another world. Roll, ye waves, roll!
Roll on unto that distant, boundless space! The soul
   But longs to sail beyond the ascending, holy mount—
Be still, my soul, and cherish these hushed words of ole:
   "To find the Truth, drink from Imagination's fount."

The Titan's Goblet by Thomas Cole, 19 3/8 x 16 1/8 in., oil on canvas, 1833, exhibited at The Metropolitan Museum of Art, New York City.

Letters We Wrote

dedicated to Diane Fournier

by Tonya McQuade

Across the months of summer and the states,
We wrote our lengthy letters, wrote our lives—
Descriptions of our summer days and dates,
Each to our mailbox drawn like bees to hives.
We wrote our girlish gossip so that we
Might keep our friendship fast though miles apart;
We wrote our hopes and dreams of what might be,
Our thoughts, concerns, and what lay on our heart.
Each summer, while in Yellowstone, she wrote;
And I, in Antioch, would do the same.
Whoever wrote the longest then would gloat!
My thirty-eight-page letter won the game.
I'm glad we could not text or email then:
I treasure all those letters writ by pen.

Clouds

a pantoum in iambic pentameter

by Dusty Grein

Clouds drift across the peaceful azure sky.
As I sit quietly under this tree,
I think of life's big questions and then sigh.
I wonder if someday I'll truly see.

As I sit quietly under this tree,
the sun is shining warm upon my face.
I wonder if someday I'll truly see
the beauty hidden deep inside this place.

The sun is shining warm upon my face.
I stretch out, gladly soaking up the light,
the beauty hidden deep inside this place,
as arms of golden warmth embrace me tight.

I stretch out, gladly soaking up the light.
I think of life's big questions and then sigh;
as arms of golden warmth embrace me tight,
clouds drift across the peaceful azure sky.

Late Winter Sunset

written on Two Tree Island, England

by M.P. Lauretta

The golden fingers of the setting sun
bestow their last caresses for the day.
Although this present day may be undone,
the sun will rise tomorrow come what may.

Now Fauna's rich diurnal paradigm
enjoys a frolic just before bedtime:

A rowdy choir of geese sings far away,
elsewhere two croaking crows stake out their turf.
A pensive curlew slowly stalks his prey,
his curious angled limbs wading the surf.

An egret inconspicuously walks by,
two mallards are already bedding down.
The distant floating gulls still play and cry
a little, but are also settling down.

This picture postcard's finely choreographed
by Nature's great circadian stagecraft.

The golden fingers of the setting sun,
their work completed, begin to pull away.
Although the present day is now undone,
the sun will rise tomorrow come what may.

II. LOVE POEMS

Cat and Claret by Steven Seward, 26 x 34 in.,
home-ground oil paints on acrylic canvas, 1995.

Love's Refrain

for Elizabeth

by Joseph Charles MacKenzie

My morning's mountain wears the lavish light
Of candid clouds and truth-engendered white.
Ah, heavens, spread your opalescent ray,
And open earth-blind eyes to boundless sight,
That love abide beyond the close of day!

And sip, O buds of May, the frigid dew!
Grow fairer, earth, to our yet waking view!
Long after bones are dust, the stars will say
That we were not found faithless or untrue,
That love abide beyond the close of day!

Come, let us walk beneath our secret bower
And pause to gather every precious flower
Life's once-blown spring is gladsome to display.
The rain of grace is falling like a shower,
That love abide beyond the close of day!

Seek not the palimpsest of time to read
Nor alter what its pages have decreed.
The parchment of the past, let it decay:
Our manuscript has yet to dry. Take heed,
That love abide beyond the close of day!

When death's cold hand unstrings my song-worn lyre,
And youth's fair form lies stretch'd upon the pyre,
We two shall look across the windless bay
To catch the distant, everlasting fire,
That love abide beyond the close of day!

Sonnet XXVII

for Elizabeth

by Joseph Charles MacKenzie

As kindly cottonwoods around us rise,
Entwining wistful melodies of green,
We walk beneath our shade-entangled skies
Through gothic vaulting, hand in hand, unseen.

Through autumn's latticework of wind-chime leaves
A sowing sun casts broad its final rays.
Soft evening bundles all our cares in sheaves
As we set forth upon our path of days.

I am the bosque, thou the breeze,
Along the Rio Grande's storied stream.
Thou art the light, and I the trees,
And our enchanted path a waking dream.

Time's river these, our days, shall not erase,
Beneath the God-made bridge of our embrace.

The Swallows of La Cienega

for Elizabeth

by Joseph Charles MacKenzie

La Cienega slept on a muted afternoon
At old *Las Golodrinas*, when I spied a nest
Of swallows beneath the age-worn *latias*, hewn
By a hand that is gone with the days that were blessed;

And I promised to knit for you a pair of gloves
From the cotton that falls from the cottonwood trees
Like the snows of *antaño*, and send them with doves
Through your heart's open window on late summer's breeze;

And to make for you the finest purse from the skin
Of the coy trout that feed on the soft floating seeds
That fall on the river, to put my sonnets in
With a Rosary of the bluest turquoise beads;

And to go up the ancient ladder very high,
Atop *el torreon*, to catch a roving cloud
And gently wrap it in an azure sheet of sky
To place beneath your feet as proof of love avowed;

And from the golden light of the adobe's straw
To fashion for your head a magnificent crown
Surmounted with crystals I saved from winter's thaw,
And sew from veils of desert rain your satin gown.

But when the swallows of La Cienega return,
And the *acequias* are full with summer's stream,
And the still marshes grow dense with cattail and fern,
You shall wake me, from this and every idle dream.

Latias: Lateral wooden slats that form part of the ceiling of a traditional New Mexican building. *Antaño*: Yesteryear. *Torreon*: A lookout tower made of adobe used to guard a settlement or watch for the arrival of wagon trains coming up the Camino Real. *Acequias*: Man-made irrigation ditches for farming.

The Day Will Come

by Jeffrey Essmann

The day will come when Beauty is restored
to us, so quietly yet utterly
beside itself our famished eyes will toward
its giddy silence barely turn to see.
But of a sudden purple tulips on
a May-lit morn a deeper bloom will don;
a cricket chirping 'neath the hush of rain
will take on tones of heavenly refrain.
When Beauty's finally had enough and casts
away its shackles forged of intellect and will,
we'll feel again the human body thrill
and know the grayness in our soul has passed.
And on that day when Beauty sings its song
I'll whisper how I've loved you all along.

In Memory of Romeo and Juliet

by Victor Tyne (high school poet)

These twain ephem'ral lives were fraught with woes
When they, a boy and girl in morn of life,
Defied their due inheritance as foes
And chased a star-crossed love as man and wife.
Belovèd by their family, kin, and friends,
To honest, faithful vow of love they swore;
Walked fortune's path to meet their self-willed ends
That ended ancient hate and true peace bore.
Each fain would drink the pois'nous sip of death
Or by the sting of dagger sharp depart,
For entering the grave's eternal rest
Proved better than to live with broken heart.
The sword of fatal love spared neither child,
But through their deaths were households reconciled.

The Youngest Rose

by Joe Tessitore

The youngest rose,
a single tear,
the pain she knows
that draws me near.

Within me grows
the need to share;
Should I expose
how much I care?

And so it goes
this summer morn
emotion flows
pricked by the thorn.

I Think of You, My Bright-Eyed Girl

by William Krusch

When the rosy light glints o'er white sand
   Of meadowlands by a shore,
When balmy zephyrs kiss the land
   Which birds and roe adore,
When a dreamy child takes rope in hand
   And quickly grabs hold the oar,
     I think of you, my bright-eyed girl,
     Illustrious one—my orient pearl.

When the gilded light o'er myrtles glows
   In myriad shining rays,
When gentle breeze of summer blows
   Across the gloaming bays,
When a babbling brook through meads e'er flows
   In splendidly warmèd days,
     I think of you, my bright-eyed girl,
     Illustrious one—my orient pearl.

When the amber leaf drops from the tree
   Midst crystalline auburn lights,
When rumbling winds from distant sea
   Now herald swallows' flights,
When the pilot thinks to face or flee
   Tempestuous stormy nights,
     I think of you, my bright-eyed girl,
     Illustrious one—my orient pearl.

When the groves are bare and gray the brake
   And heavily falls the hail,
When roaring gales have come to take
   The ship from off its trail,
When the sun has set beneath the lake
   Where souls of the valiant sail,
      I think of you, my bright-eyed girl,
      Illustrious one—my orient pearl.

When across the earth I've traveled far
   In search of the True, the One,
When found that I've sailed o'er the bar,
   And find the journey done,
When in calm repose I watch each star,
   Each heavenly glowing sun,
      I see you now, my bright-eyed girl,
      Illustrious one—eternal gold pearl.

Joy Comes

by Rachel Holbrook

Softly silent; kindly kept,
   the haunted hours crept.
Moonlit minutes—marked and mute,
   the lonely doubt takes root.
The tendrils twine; the rootlets reach.
   Somehow the sun must breach.
Morning breaks; my bridegroom's come—
   virtue's vigil done.
The light of love shines stronger still.
   Awake, Amore's thrill!

'Cause You'll Be Here

by Gleb Zavlanov

The butterfly, the sea anemone,
And snowflake, though possessive of the true
Design of grace and perfect symmetry,
Seem crude and ugly when compared to you.
The stars that line the deep, black sky like grains
Of salt, the sun that ripens like a peach,
The Northern Lights that brighten arctic plains
With swirling luminescence; though they each
Shine bright, there's not a light as bright as yours
To clear the shadows roosting in my breast,
To lighten up my mood when life grows worse,
And put my worries and my fears to rest.
And even if the world collapses in
Dense shadow, and those lights just disappear,
The world will be as it has always been:
The world won't lose a thing 'cause you'll be here.

Portrait of Monsieur de Lavoisier and his Wife, chemist Marie-Anne Pierrette Paulze by Jacques-Louis David, 102.2 x 76.6 in., oil on canvas, 1788, exhibited at The Metropolitan Museum of Art, New York City.

Three Loves in One

by C.B. Anderson

We've gathered Love, but only insofar
As we have reaped a crop from seeds we've sown.
Those hours we cherished our beloved are
The most rewarding times we've ever known,
Which bears a certain similarity
To what occurs through strangers we behold:
Each freely given act of charity
Repays the helping hand one hundred-fold.

Philosophers love wisdom more than knowledge
And prove it when they strive to know themselves
As thoroughly as facts they learned in college
From dusty books arrayed on crowded shelves.

Give love away to everyone you meet,
And let your heart thereby be made complete.

III. HUMOR

Whimsy by Steven J. Levin, 28 x 20 in., oil on canvas, 2013.
Courtesy of Cavalier Galleries, New York.

Computer Worship

from A Gallery of Ethopaths

by Joseph S. Salemi

The computer is a simple tool—
It cannot change an arrant fool
Into a brilliant, thoughtful scholar,
Although the damned thing costs top-dollar.
It cannot help someone to write
Whose prose is just a total blight
Nor delineate a topic
For someone naturally myopic.
It cannot give poetic insight
To someone with a mental dim-light.
People who say the thing "inspires"
Are brain-dead, ethopathic liars—
You might as well say that a quill
Gave Shakespeare intellect and will
To write his sonnets, pen his plays,
Or inkwells spouted Shelley's lays,
Or that old Vergil's iron stylus
Taught him the words that still beguile us.
Do you attribute skill to Dante
Because he had some parchment handy?
And yet you think a P.C.'s blinking
Helps to develop human thinking,
Or that a "Spell-Check" is a boon
To some illiterate buffoon
Who has no style, no grace, no credence,
And can't keep track of antecedents.

Persons who know computers well
Have no use for the hyped-up sell
That cyber-freaks are ever spouting.
They say that, beyond all doubting,
Computer software can't imbue
A booby with a new I.Q.
For if you are a stupid schmuck
Computers cannot change your luck,
And if your mental level's zero
Computers won't make you a hero.
Consult the experts once again—
It's true with P.C.s as with men.
This maxim holds, without a doubt:
That *garbage in* means *garbage out.*
So don't tell me because you got a
Macintosh your prose is hotter;
Or that you now can write like Pinter
Because you have a laser printer.
Don't confuse things instrumental
With matters that are elemental.
Great art comes from those fair Muses
Crackling through your psychic fuses
And not through microchips and wire
Sold at prices ever higher.
This is a myth to make gods chortle:
That simple circuitry's immortal—
A thing believed by addlepates,
Weirdos, morons, or Bill Gates.

Let's Take the Other Bus

A Liberal-Socialist Primer for Our Youngest, Most Impressionable Comrades

by Amy Foreman

Come gather round me, little ones:
you bourgeois girls, suburban sons.
I am your teacher, leader, czar;
get on my bus and we'll go far.

America is wrong, you see,
and none of you are really free
when rich kids all across this land
have candy, toys, and cash in hand.

Those evil, wealthy, nasty brats
(not one, a child of Democrats),
they make your lives unhappy, poor;
How can you smile when they have more?

Sweet Susie, dear, what's that you said?
You don't believe that God is dead?
Your daddy said that you should pray?
Oh, dear young Susie, keep away

from evil men who try to teach
you patriarchal, hate-filled speech,
for God is mean and horrible,
and daddies are deplorable.

(That means they're bad, young Susie, dear,
so don't repeat their words in here.
Especially, don't say, "my dad,"
or little Johnny might be sad.

See, Johnny can't quite understand
that "Dad" word that our school has banned
since both his moms have tried to stress
that parent roles are gender-less.)

Yes, Johnny? You were wondering
about colonial plundering?
Let's talk about that, children dear,
for it's a sordid tale you'll hear:

The men who tamed this wilderness
were villains all, I must confess.
They brought the smallpox, don't forget,
and chopped down trees and were a threat

to every wolf and buffalo;
they ruined Mother Earth, you know.
Each racist-bigot-homophobe,
still threatens life around the globe.

So, children, we must join as one
to overturn what they have done.
We'll fight for redistributing
the toys to which rich children cling.

We'll fight to end all fatherhood
and girlhood, boyhood, too—we should.
We'll fight and yell with all our might
that right is wrong and wrong is right.

No God or family, not for us:
we're all aboard the liberal bus!

*Note: "take the other bus" is a slang
term for homosexual behavior.*

75

Time for the B.S.

Susie and Johnny Go to College

by Amy Foreman

Welcome, young friends, to this great university.
I am your counselor, Dr. Diversity,
here to advise you on all of your classes and
campus life, brimming with fun and perversity.

Visit our Safe Spaces in every lecture hall:
personal havens from real or conjectural
concepts that trigger you, things you don't understand,
right-wing, offensive, or just architectural.

Here you'll meet like-minded students (no scrutiny);
here you can orchestrate riots and mutiny,
easily shutting down lectures the school has planned,
joining together in radical unity.

As to your classes: they've changed quite substantially,
now that Red China supports us financially.
Once we taught Plato, the Sciences, Civics and
History, Grammar, Linguistics, all agilely.

Not anymore. Now it's Gender Fluidity,
Feminist Lit'rature, Rainbow Identity,
Marxism 101, Eco-Oppression and
Queer Theory: all to ensure your tumidity.

Moving along: here's our Campus Dispensary.
Stop in today to explore every sensory
pleasure without any price-tag, you understand:
name-brand protection for everyone, all for free!

And if, perchance, a young hedonist undergrad
slips up and gets a girl pregnant, it ain't so bad.
Screenings, "Plan B," and abortions (all in demand)
terminate "aftereffects" of the fun you had.

Follow me quickly now: time for your parents to
cough up their money to cover the payments due.
They'll be delighted to place you in our command,
knowing our duty's to educate students who

hate the establishment: anarchist militants,
fragile young libertines, hooked on their stimulants,
gender-less profligates, each one a firebrand,
delicate, soft, unemployable dissidents.

Snowflake "adults" who can't handle adversity:
that's who we train up at this university!

Check-Mate by a Pawn

for my sons

by Amy Foreman

We parry, thrust:
This game of wits,
Where each pawn must
Deflect your hits.

My mounted knight
Skips overhead,
First back, then right;
Your knight is dead.

But you riposte,
With bishop swift,
My rook, engrossed,
Forgets to shift.

And then, I spot
A yawning crack,
The perfect shot
For my attack.

I strike so hard
At your regime,
But you bombard
Each best-laid scheme.

We soldier forth
To launch each quest,
From South to North,
And East to West.

Until it's down
To king and queen,
To seize the crown:
A dreadful scene.

You're cornered now;
You have no chance.
Or, … anyhow,
Not at first glance.

But then one pawn,
Forgotten, small,
Advances on
My castle wall.

He checks my king
And wins the game;
Oh, what a sting
When pawn's to blame

The Execution by Jacob A. Pfeiffer, 6 x 8 in., oil on panel, 2009.

Untamed Daughter

"…come, Kate, come, you must not look so sour."
—The Taming of the Shrew

by A.M. Juster

At fourteen she loves being critical
and tells me, "Shakespeare uses language well,
but could have been, like, more original…"
I sputter, but rebuttals fail to jell.
All those recycled plots make it appear
to her he was a sneaky plagiarist—
no better than that girl expelled last year—
so "they" should take him off her reading list.

Please, Caitlin, let it go; great writers borrow
like gamblers. Don't begrudge the Bard a source
that he reshaped into Verona's sorrow,
Miranda's tenderness or Lear's remorse,
but mark him down at least a point or two
because he tamed a Kate as fierce as you.

First appeared in The Formalist *Vol 14 Issue 2, 2003*

The Choice Is Yours

by C.L. Clickard

There are kingdoms to rule if your foot's the right size
    or your beauty is flawless and rare.
With a tune and a tower, you'll capture brave hearts—
    if you don't mind his boots in your hair.

Kiss the beast or the frog and you'll set a prince free.
    (He's a jerk, but he's mended his ways.)
When you meet a sleek wolf on the road to your Gran's
    keep those goodies tucked safely away

Hah!

Sure, Princessing RULES, but some princes are fools.
    Don't swallow your pride or your voice.
Should you happily ever? Or happily never?
    No one else has the right—it's YOUR choice.

Take that sword off the shelf and go rescue yourself.
    Dump the frogs. Face a dragon or two.
Be clever and brave! There's a world to be saved.
    The fairy tale hero is YOU.

The Fiancé

inspired by Anthony Trollope's
"Can you forgive her?" *(1864–1865)*

by Sheri-Ann O'Shea

Alice, he wants your money, honey.
Alice, he wants your cash.
He'd never ask you without it
don't doubt it—
He's wild; but that would be rash.

He's no use for Alice in theory, dearie;
He's no use for Alice in fact.
So don't throw your heart in
it hasn't a part in
The requisite terms of the pact.

Every man has a sweetheart, sweetheart,
Every man has a pet
This man is in love with himself
and your pelf
Is all that he's anxious to get.

Political Correctness

after Joachim du Bellay's "Les Regrets LXVIII"

by Margaret Coates

I hate the Florentines' foul avarice,
I hate lewd Sienese profanity,
I hate Geneva's glib duplicity,
I hate malign Venetian artifice,
I hate whate'er Ferrara does amiss,
I hate the Lombards' infidelity
And Neapolitan diversity,
And lazy Rome's loquacious cowardice.
I hate how the English smirk, and Scotsmen cheat,
How Burgundy betrays France indiscreet,
How Spaniards strut, and drunken Germans balk,
And I who hate some vice in every nation
Renounce political equivocation,
For most of all I hate how pundits talk.

Here Comes the Hybrid Bus

by K.G. Jackson

Here comes that brand new hybrid bus
Round the street so pretty;
Its length so long it makes the turn,
And bends right round the city.

It's certainly looking very clean,
All spick-and-span and bright;
Too bad that not a single soul
Is riding it tonight!

Boasted Viridian

by Alexander King Ream

Said Viridian Green to Cerulean Blue,
"The waves would be boring without me and you,
The crashing unflashing, the sheen without glow,
Silver unplugged: not luminous, Bro."

Three Limericks

by Nivedita Karthik

An acrobat named Larry Loops
was best among all circus troupes,
But he quit one day
and was heard to say,
"My boss made me jump all those hoops!"

~

There once was a man from Keele
who slipped on an orange peel.
He fractured his foot
and was told to stay put
on account of his Achilles' heel.

~

There was a young lady named Lottie
Whose sneaking was so very naughty.
She met Geraldine
Who was in quarantine
And came back to home red and spotty.

In the Poetry Writing Workshop

"Milton conceived the Paradise Lost as a whole before he executed it in portions. We have his own authority also for the Muse having 'dictated'to him the 'unpremeditated song', and let this be answer to those who would allege the fifty-six various readings of the first line of the Orlando Furioso. Compositions so produced are to poetry what mosaic is to painting."
—*Percy Bysshe Shelley*, A Defence of Poetry

by William Ruleman

"Consider your poem a mosaic,"
Said the well-meaning poet-critic.
Well, I'd paid for his advice,
And he acted kind of nice,
Though when I saw him regale
That blond and buxom female,
I knew she would be his star.
He'd take her, yes, and far.

"What? Poetry—emotion?
Where'd you get that notion?
Eliot tells us 'feeling.'
Just don't send our senses reeling.
And what? You said inspiration?
Be wary of sudden sensation.
How much would it trouble you
To follow Richard W.?
A poem is like a fine wine,
Nuances in every line.
If you grasp all at once,
It must be the work of a dunce.
A poem should not mean but be.
Will I have to give you a C?"

Well, all this seemed fine and good.
I said that I'd understood.
But what of the mind's "fading coal"
And the God-besotted soul?
In my ear whispered Shelley:
"This fellow's a nervous Nellie."

*Richard W.: Richard Wilbur (1921–2017), a poet who
still used traditional forms and techniques.*

The Journey

by Joe Tessitore

My train of thought rolls down the track,
I know it's never coming back.
The station master waves good-bye,
a single tear falls from his eye.
The whistle blows, she rounds the bend,
the signal of my journey's end.
I do not grieve, I don't regret,
I take my leave, and I forget.

This Sonnet Has Been Funded by the State

by Jeffrey Essmann

This sonnet has been funded by the State
despite the fact it has no axe to grind.
I really looked for something I could hate,
but MSNBC's all I could find.
Upfront I ought to mention that I'm white,
and worse: a man, but in defense I'd say
I'm fairly nice and terribly polite
and told the arts committee I was gay.
The chair (a gender quite beyond all guess)
unsubtly suggested my work show
how rhyme supports the fascist status quo.
And though no whore for money, I confess
that if with State approval I am crowned,
I may become the liberals' Ezra Pound.

Whatever Is, Is Right

…a contemporary application of Pope's wisdom

by Don Shook

I've sent illegal immigrants
to splash around your pool,
to raid your pantry, watch TV,
because I know you're cool.
They'll realize you're not upset
by sharing your success;
that you are fair and really care,
and not the least distressed.
Next week I'm sending twenty more.
This group is unemployed;
but they don't care, because welfare
ensures they're overjoyed.
Still, they don't have as much as you,
so you must distribute
your bank account for an amount
that's more or less acute.
And then there are the homeless ones
who'll be there in two weeks
to share your bed and in your stead
they'll kiss your rosy cheeks;
for they will have as much as you
and you will have the same,
the justice that you voted for…
so really, who's to blame?

You can fool some of the people…

The Fall

by Jenni Wyn Hyatt

Now, if you're sitting comf'tably,
then listen to my ballad;
it is a Summer evening tale
of pizza and of salad.

"I'll take the plates out, love," I said,
for your hands tend to shake,
but I am steadier and I'd hate
the crockery to break.

The threshold proved my downfall—I'm
not sure what happened there,
but suddenly I found myself
in transit through the air.

A plate went flying from my grasp;
I heard a sickening sound
and turned to see the china spread
in pieces on the ground.

My pizza lay in disarray—
condemn me if you must—
I grieved more for my olives which
were rolling in the dust.

Meanwhile, and somewhat overcome,
I lay there in a huddle.
Was I in need of ambulance
Or just a hubby cuddle?

We checked and found me shaken,
more than usually dazed,
but only with a twisted foot,
a hand and elbow grazed.

We shared the unspoilt pizza and
the salad bowl was fine,
but all clouds have a lining so
we drank our fill of wine!

Banquet Still Life by Adriaen van Utrecht,
72.8 x 95.4 in., oil on canvas, 1644., detail.

Art

by Phillip Whidden

Why photograph a fact when you can catch
A nightmare, be a Jackson Pollock or
A Dalí at his Druid weirdest? Snatch
A depth of fanged subconscious and then pour
Some paint of guts across your canvas. Real
Is boring. Ditch it. Art becomes mirage
And mystic queasiness inside a squeal.
Eschew the common or make a collage
Of it that churns up nausea. The key
Trick is to mix up meaning or to ban
It. Spread some purple fantasy and brie
Across a beach. Jesus on a divan
With hydrogen bomb mushroom clouds would do
Or cover some swallows with Elmer's Glue.

Pentadactyl

*A 5-foot dactylic poem with a truncated
fifth foot on the odd-numbered lines.
(With apologies to Pterodactyls.)*

by Joe Spring

Dactyls are terrible lizards that fly at the mind
pounding their emphasis boldly, Jurassical pelicans
dipping through breakers, the roaring of others behind,
beating Tithonian wings like the rotors of helicons.

Such a great leathery creature with talons will bind
even the boldest of poets, who long for a particle,
something more gentle to bring in a beautiful line...
Dactyls deny any space for an opening article.

Forgive Me, Dactyl

by Joe Spring

Thinking again about dactyls and how they don't tolerate
stress out of place or the sneaky insertion of syllables,
gladly and humbly I wonder, perhaps I should moderate
poetry calling them dinosaurs, bigots, and imbeciles.

P'raps we should think of a dactyl as champion of chastity,
raising the banner of vehement structural sanctity,
hating the sin of iambic compulsion of poetry,
leading the poet in pathways of diligent purity.

Questatements

by Alessio Zanelli

If seasons pass too fast you'd better run.
If they proceed too slow indulge in fun.

Sunups are best enjoyed in days of cold.
Sundowns when heat waves linger fierce and bold.

Old age returns all that you thought was lost.
Except perennial snow and springtime frost.

Dost thou remember some of William's verse?
The Proverbs telling what to bless or curse?

Worse lines are surely jotted down today.
And yet the ink invades the page to stay.

I Taught a Lesson to My Toes

by David Watt

I taught a lesson to my toes,
They'd overstepped the mark,
Escaping time and time again
From nylon prisons dark.

I warned them of the consequence
Should they destroy more socks—
I'd bare them to the public gaze,
Like prisoners in stocks.

With feet made bare, exposed to air,
I bid their soles repent;
And without ends to tunnel through
Their wiggles proved misspent.

But as the winter chill approached
I softened my resolve,
Declaring: "My offenders ten,
With fresh socks I absolve!"

Sail Fever

by David Watt

I knew some terms, the merest germs
Of illness called 'Sail Fever':
Tack starboard, port, keep mainsail taut,
Steer boat by tiller lever!

One Saturday, beside the bay,
A salesman full of running
Cast practiced spiel of salty zeal,
Sheer confidence and cunning.

He said, "This boat will stay afloat
Through any storm or bluster,
And in the main, she won't complain,
No matter skills you muster.

Commanding crew of one or two,
They'll call you Captain, Sir!
With Captain's hat, windblown cravat—
A sight to make one stir!

In years ahead, when home in bed,
You'll love your purchase bold;
A bargain bought, Life's high-tides caught!
(May I mark as SOLD?)"

I met defeat, not through deceit,
But pitch designed most clever;
The pull of sea to large degree,
A dream of sails forever.

About to gloat, with sailing boat,
A bill of sale to show it;
There came a thought of some import—
I had no means to tow it!

Out on a Limb

by David Watt

In an old timber town lived a man of renown;
With a chainsaw he couldn't be beat,
And as quick as you'd say "What's for dinner today?"
Limbs would fall, cut precise and complete;
And when challengers came, they departed in shame,
With their heads hanging down in defeat.

Charles Magee was his name, though because of his fame,
He was known more as 'Chainsaw Magee.'
But 'Old-Timers' deplored the way that he sawed
With a motorized means to cut tree.
So they worked up a plan, soon agreed to a man—
It was cunning, as cruelty can be.

They said, "To be fair, as you're high in the air,
We can't tell if you're cutting correct,
So climb out to the tip—don't be giving us lip!—
From out there your prowess we'll detect;
And be certain to smile as you're cutting in style,
For the newspapers, council elect."

And so came the day when the town in dismay
Saw Magee of fast chainsaw fall flat,
When out of pride he cut limb on inside,
Fell to earth with a sickening splat!
And now etched in tree, sage advice states for free:
"When you're out on a limb use a mat!"

In Praise of Lovely Homes

by Janice Canerdy

Relaxing on the porch as darkness fell,
I sipped iced tea, reflecting on my day.
There was breathtaking beauty all around,
the perfect lawn, a pleasure to survey.

I'd had a scrumptious meal with fine red wine
and watched a Lifetime romance on TV.
I'd waltzed around the den as CDs played
the tunes I love the best by Kenny G.

Then came my thirty-minute bubble bath,
so warm and soothing. While still damp, I lay,
just briefly, on the comfy bed. I dressed
and used a lightly scented body spray.

That's when I got the tea and came outside
to relish what should be the best of nights.
Euphoria was at a height—AND THEN
IT STOPPED! I saw two brightly glaring lights.

The Johnsons, owners of the house, were back
two days before they were supposed to be!
I tossed the tea glass in a well-pruned shrub
and fled before they got a glimpse of me.

The Blakes' weeklong vacation will begin
tomorrow. Like the Johnsons, they will hide
their house key in a fake rock near the porch.
Man, I can hardly wait to get inside!

'Round Bedtime

a villanelle for my daughter

by Tim J. Myers

When will sleep subdue this noisy cub?
It's 10 p.m., but still she wants to take
her seventy-one-piece tea set in the tub.

This is what she wants, and here's the rub:
Until she's all played out she'll stay awake.
Oh when will sleep subdue this noisy cub?

She'll scream if I (before that final glub
of water down the drain) should undertake
to lift her precious tea set from the tub.

She's belting out a tuneless rub-a-dub—
the tiles echo till my eardrums ache.
Oh when will sleep subdue this noisy cub?

I might assuage my dolor at the pub,
but cannot here shake off the urge to break
her seventy-one-piece tea set in the tub.

She's out now, but she cries for frosted flakes.
The bathroom floor's an unnamed little lake.
Oh when will sleep subdue this noisy cub?
I fish her floating tea things from the tub.

The Attic War

by James A. Tweedie

A squirrel moved into my house
And claimed my attic for his summer home.
At first, I thought it was a mouse
That nibbled on my insulation foam.

Outside my window I could see
Him gather pine nuts for his winter stash,
Not knowing at the time that he
Was sneaking in my roof to hide the cache.

Evicting him was hard to do;
He had, it seemed, the law upon his side.
For using poison was taboo—
I.e., roast peanuts laced with cyanide.

For every hole I blocked, he found
Two others he could use to enter in.
Holes in the eaves, holes in the ground,
He was a break-in artist veteran.

His midnight scratching drove me mad,
His cleverness upset me all the more.
I failed with every plan I had.
It wasn't just a nuisance, it was war!

It took two months to win the fight.
He chewed through wire mesh and steel wool
Until I locked him out one night
By stuffing foil into every hole.

I won the war but to this day
I'm wary of that squirrel who did me wrong.
And though he now tucks nuts away
And stores them in a tree where they belong

I worry that he still recalls
Those nuts he piled so neatly in a stack
Behind my upstairs bedroom walls…
And that he has a plan to get them back.

Dulation

by James A. Tweedie

The word "dulation" I find most amusing;
A word I've never been accused of using.
It's not a verb (objective or subjective),
It's not a noun, or even an adjéctive.
It's not a word at all, apparently.
It isn't listed in the OED.
"Dulation" by itself is most absurd.
But if you add a prefix? It's a word!
It seems this non-word can find abrogation
When it appears in the word "a-dulation."
It also can be found in its negation
When it appears in the word "un-dulation."
If someone could define the word "dulation,"
I'd use it gladly without hesitation.

OED: Oxford English Dictionary

There Are No Long-Term Consequences When the End Is Near!

by Lee Goldberg

A wondrous thing that happens as your exit becomes near,
is that "long-term" consequences need not cause you fear!

Bottom line: there's no "long-term" when soon you'll meet your savior!
The construct becomes meaningless, so why restrain behavior?

Melanoma matters not, go bask in the bright sun.
Enjoy your favorite cigarette after the tanning's done.

Who cares if cholesterol results in heart disease?
Eat that double bacon-burger with some extra cheese!

Catch and cook those tasty fish from that polluted river.
Drink away the hours each day. To hell with your dumb liver!

Send a naughty picture to your hot neighbor's email.
You'll be underground before she gets you thrown in jail.

Grab that balding pudgy chap and yank off his dumb rug!
Overdo your meds and get real high on some good drug.

Practice techniques with a pro until they are perfected.
Do it fast and do it slow and do it unprotected!

I swear to you that I did live the things that I now preach.
I can guarantee the same joys are within your reach!

Just avoid my one faux pas. Don't start at twenty-five.
(I would be thirty-two today if I were still alive.)

Ode to the Lats

by Connie Phillips

Oh Lat, dear Lat, where art thou at?
Methinks thou seem a bit too flat…
On Superman, and blokes like that,
Your rippling mass is no doormat!

With Arnold, Dwayne the Rock, and Hulk,
The goal has been to build more bulk:
No pain no gain—don't sit and sulk,
To suffer is to see results!

Latissimus, Latissimus,
You surely have our backs, and thus
To stretch and strengthen is a must.
No weight is e'er superfluous!

Latissimi are where it's at…
Alas, my lats are none but fat!

Lat: Latissimus dorsi muscle. A muscle connecting
the upper extremity to the vertebral column.

The Anchor

after Edgar Allan Poe's "The Raven"

by Steven Shaffer

Once upon an evening dreary, I searched for news, at least in theory,
Over many a dubious and mendacious channel that I abhor—
While I surfed, nearly barfing, suddenly there came a harping,
There was someone roughly berating, berating everything I stand for.
"'Tis some moron," I muttered, "blabbing on this channel poor—
    Only this and nothing more."

Ah, distinctly I remember, it was such-and-so "News Center";
And each separate vying member wrought opinion upon the floor.
Eagerly I wished for pausing; a painful headache it was causing
From incessant babbling—babbling for the lost tenor—
For the rare and radiant moment which the ratings most adore—
    Stop them falling through the floor.

And the speakers—strangely certain, rushing to get a bit of dirt in
Chilled me—filled me with revulsions never felt before;
So that now, to still the pounding in my head, I sat entreating
"No more pundits spewing senseless manure!
Another useless pundit spewing senseless manure!
    I can't take this anymore."

Presently my soul grew stronger; hesitating then no longer,
"Sir," tweet I, "or Madam, truly your forgiveness I implore;
But the fact is I was watching, and so rashly you kept talking,
And so loudly you kept talking, talking about ideas I deplore,
I checked for sure I heard you right—is this what you stand for?"
    Bias there and nothing more.

Deep into that bias sinking, long their logic twisting, resisting,
Any reasoned idea a mortal ever dared to have before;
But with platitudes unbroken, not a reasoned word was spoken,
And requests for balance, at least token, was retorted with "What for?"
I asked for fairness, and an echo murmured back to me, "What for?"
    Merely this and nothing more.

Back into the channels tuning, all my soul within me burning,
Soon again I heard gums flapping even louder than before.
"Surely," said I, "surely this is something worth watching;
Let me see, then, if not CNN, this other station to explore—
Let my heart be still a moment and this station to explore—
      'Tis MSNBC and nothing more!"

Over there I flung the remote, my annoyance thus to denote,
I was now a captive watcher, on that station evermore;
Not a single dial on the TV, no button from which this channel to flee,
But, with mien of lord or lady, perched at a desk without a drawer—
Perched at a desk, but we can't see the floor—
      Sat the anchor, and nothing more.

Then this anchor, never smiling, always papers shuffling and piling,
By the grave and stern decorum of the countenance it wore,
"With thy head so shorn and shaven, thou," I said, "art sure no maven,
Ghastly grim, as though the whole world was at war—
Tell me when some positive news you will finally explore!"
      Quoth the anchor, "Nevermore."

Much I marveled this ungainly crier to hear discourse so plainly,
Though its answer little meaning—little relevancy bore;
For I cannot help agreeing that we should all be fleeing
This anchor I was seeing, welcome as a cold sore—
Opinions as deep and thoughtful as a college sophomore,
      I wish to see it nevermore.

But the anchor, sitting lonely at the placid desk, spoke only
But one word, as if its soul in that one word it did outpour.
We would all be ushered, to the truth in one word: "Russia"-
As if holding fast the key that could feed and clothe all the world's poor-
When oh when will you stop speaking, when oh when say it no more?
      Quoth the anchor, "Nevermore."

But the anchor still jolting all my brain cells to revolting,
Straight I wheeled a cushioned seat to block the eyesore;
Then, with continued hearing, my ears were nearly bleeding,
Repeating "Russia Russia Russia," I wondered what for—
What this grim, ungainly, ghastly, gaunt Babylonian whore
      Meant in croaking "Nevermore."

And the anchor, still chattering, still is sitting, still is sitting
On the pallid Farnsworth tube, set on a stand from the store;
And its eyes have all the seeming of a demon's that is dreaming,
And the LED o'er it streaming throws its shadow on the floor;
In some other soul's TV room, not mine anymore,
    I shall be watching—nevermore!

From the Shortest Poem Contest

Cheesemaking

Find a way
To weigh
The whey.

—Ben Foreman, Cascabel, Arizona

Trip of a Lifetime

The place within.
Shall we begin?

—James B. Nicola, New York, New York

Homeric Hymns*

A Homer
misnomer.

—J. Simon Harris, Raleigh, North Carolina
*Footnote: the Homeric hymns were probably not written by Homer.

Martyr's Imperative

I
Die.

—Juleigh Howard-Hobson, Cascadia, USA

IV. EXPOSING
COMMUNISM

The Great Red Dragon and the Woman Clothed with the Sun by William Blake
15.7 x 12.7 in., watercolor painting, circa 1805–1810.

Arise, You Bones

"Come, spirit, from the four winds, and blow
upon these slain, and let them live again."
–Ezechiel 37:9

by Adam Sedia

Arise, you bones of millions, scattered far,
Half-buried, all forgotten, that remain
From the red dragon and its blood-stained star,
That crushed near half the world beneath its reign,
Raged, overthrew, and waged eternal war
On truth and light, the decent and the sane—

You bones of martyrs slain for faith confessed;
Of kings and princes slaughtered for your birth;
Of peasants starved as theory put to test;
Of myriad young, old, women, men, your worth
Naught but what blood and toil brute force could wrest,
Like cattle herded, like chaff dumped in earth.

Arise from every gulag-dotted land:
From windswept Arctic tundra, Yakut woods,
Wide Kazakh steppes, and searing Turkmen sand;
From blood-soaked rice-fields where the Yangtze floods
And where the spires of glorious Angkor stand;
From mine-sown jungles where war's shade yet broods.

Arise! Assemble, joint connecting joint
Into a deathless host of millions strong;
Surge forth in righteous wrath; seize sword, spear-point;
Mow down the dragon, reigning still so long,
The mobs it spawned, the lords it dared anoint;
Avenge at last your unrequited wrong!

Charge through the ivied academic halls
Where yet the dragon spins its fantasies;
Charge through the presses, studios, and malls,
Where yet its tongue spews countless lies with ease;

Charge through the domes of scattered capitals
Where yet its greedy talons crush and seize.

Avenge your blood, your chains, your stifled souls,
And make an unmoved world at last atone.
Your cause is just; its hour of vengeance tolls.
You had no Nuremberg, now make your own.
No army freed you; form a tide that rolls
Worldwide and crashes on foes overthrown.

To Xi

by Adam Sedia

Do you not hear them, Chairman Xi?
Victims tied for the surgeon's blade,
Their final shrieks of agony,
Their hearts carved out and iced for trade?
Hear them, hear them, Chairman Xi!

Do you not see them, Chairman Xi?
Dismembered limbs torn from the womb,
The wailing mothers, forced to see
Their womanhood become a tomb?
See them, see them, Chairman Xi!

Do you not know them, Chairman Xi?
The prisons full of those who gazed
Past Marx and Mao to deity,
Their altars smashed, their temples razed?
Know them, know them, Chairman Xi!

Do you not fear them, Chairman Xi?
The distant quakes from Tiananmen—
A people crushed, whose dignity
Demands its greatness rise again?
Fear them, fear them, Chairman Xi!

The Chinese Bill of Rights

by C.B. Anderson

In China, laws regarding human rights
May keep a simple man awake at nights,
Suspecting that a Mand'rin *guten Morgen*
Might mean the harvest of a vital organ.

Old Adolf Hitler would have found his equal
With what's played out in this Far-Eastern sequel.
The struggle's lasted many years, but now
Confirmed: the legacy of Chairman Mao.

Inside this vast "Republic of the People"
One never sees a synagogue or steeple,
And though believers there may wonder why,
The only given is the right to die.

Folks have the right to bow before the State,
And any who object have sealed their fate.
And, too, there is the right to cringe and kneel
Beneath the Party's red oppressive heel.

The innocent are always first to go;
In China, this is all you need to know.
God help you if you cleave to Falun Gong:
Your only right is to be treated wrong.

Guten Morgen: German for "good morning"

Subsidizing Poverty

When you subsidize something you get more of it.
—A fundamental law of economics

by C.B. Anderson

As Thomas Sowell has so often pointed out,
Black family units, by and large, remained intact
Before the massive Welfare System came about.
And illegitimacy then was not a fact

Of life the Government sustained with cash rewards.
Though most of us get up each day and go to work,
Could we resist the lure of prepaid smorgasbords?
And if they cut us off, would we then go berserk?

There's nothing wrong with showing sensible compassion,
But when the rats come home, just who will pay the piper?
Self-pride and self-reliance, now, are out of fashion,
And Uncle Sam has soiled himself—please change his diaper!

The Welfare check has proved sufficient to disable
The market force that once kept families whole and stable.

On the Killing of Falun Gong Mother and Child

Ms. Wang Lixuan (pronounced Wahng Leeshwahn) and her son, Meng Hao (Muhng How), were detained on Oct. 22, 2000. Mother and baby both died at the Tuanhe Forced Labor Dispatch Division in Beijing on Nov. 7, 2000. The coroner's exam determined that Ms. Wang's neck and fingers were broken, her skull was fractured, and she had a needle stuck in her lower back.

by Damian Robin

The child lies quiet. Quieter than the grave.
And still. A stillness that belongs to sleep
Where infants' bodies do not misbehave.

His mother lies beside him, parallel,
Also still—too still to be asleep,
Their limbs just so, so neat, laid out so well.

Their poses shaped by someone else's will
Who did not try to make them seem asleep,
Just not too bloody mangled—done with skill.

Yet though their clothes are placed back on their legs,
Although their eyes are closed as though in sleep,
On clotted feet and ankles are the dregs

Of metal manacles and scrapes in skin
So sinew-deep the wearer could not sleep
Unless unconscious; but they don't breathe in.

When they were breathing, both hung upside-down,
The mother manacled, the baby tied,
The skirt and clothing dangling, hanging down,

Their hair on end toward the pooling ground,
Each dropped hair thinner than the rope that tired,
Than the chain that chained. Yet they are bound

More hard than strings of DNA or love
Or twined umbilical that once had tied,
So deep inside, below the push and shove

Of daily strife, of health's mechanicals,
Of needs to which all humankind is tied
With better knowledge than mere animals.

And then the backward movement of the blood
Downward to the heads—and there it paused
Or broke through broken skin, or made a flood

In nostrils till those fonts would, breathless, clot.
Can we, right now, take in these deaths and, paused,
Consider what inhuman, demon plot

This single couple's persecution took?
There's no snuff movie footage to be paused,
No rewind showing human meat and hook,

No reasoning, except we know the cause
Was adamantine will to keep belief,
To not give up on universal laws,

Of Truth, Compassion, Tolerance, the core
Of Falun Gong; not let a spirit thief
Rip out two souls without which there's no more,

No more life, no mother and no child,
No more conscience, nothing except grief
And mindless fragmentation in the wild.

Golden Lotus by Daci Shen, 69 x 43 in., oil on canvas, 2004. This oil painting was inspired by the death of Wang Lixuan and her son in a Chinese labor camp. The Chinese characters read "Truthfulness, Compassion, and Tolerance."

An Orphan's Sorrow by Xiqiang Dong, 48 x 48 in., oil on canvas, 2006.

Hard To Believe

*Prisoners of conscience are murdered for
their organs today in communist China.*

by Damian Robin

In the West, it's hard to bond an organ—
match live human flesh—person to person—
meld—make fresh—a deeply human token,
gifting a working function to one broken.
There must be matched consent to transfer—quickly—
while loved ones love or grieve, calm or angry.
If the giver's still alive, the giving
has to leave the opened donor living
or it's probed as murder.   Yet in China,
can you believe, there is a high yield quota,
deep in poisoned stomachs of the Party,
of transferred body parts for making money,
and damping down disquiet. This state life-thieve—
death by surgery—makes good souls heave.

There Are Millions More

by Damian Robin

So here I am, slouched outside a furnace,
unclothed, untagged, my family not informed
—my treatments, interventions, they can't guess.
My muscle-freeze sets in while hell-flame-stormed
incinerators hide the bones of men
and women and children further up the queue
whose organs fed the glut of Party men
and women who push to spread the Party glue.

As I no longer hurt, don't pray for me
for I'm a stamped-out man the West's research
won't reach—but there are millions marked, go find,
at home, in jail, in bed, or walking free,
whose urine, tissue, blood, hang on a perch
and could, at any moment, be assigned.

Weaknesses

by Charlie Bauer

I read that Christ said: "Turn the other cheek,"
And told good friends I held that notion, but
Still wondered if that turning made me weak.
The answer didn't seem to be clear cut.

"I'll show you weakness," said His voice, "Just see
What blood Red China's done to those who hold
That truthfulness best defines reality,
Show mercy, practice self-control, don't fold

When they are taken, day or night, to be
Maimed, tortured, all for doing nothing wrong;
Their organs taken by Beijing's decree.
In case you wonder, they're the Falun Gong.

So if you bristle at another's reach,
Remember: others suffer what you preach."

Cell Block Twenty-Nine

by David Watt

I haven't seen the sun for days,
Nor felt Compassion's gentle ways;
My body's weak, but courage stays,
In Cell Block Twenty-Nine.

They tell me "Falun Gong's a lie!"
And if I don't renounce, I'll die
For price of liver, lung, or eye,
In Cell Block Twenty-Nine.

They type my tissue, take my blood
Until my veins refuse to flood;
And as result, I fall with thud
In Cell Block Twenty-Nine.

Please let this misery be done;
Not for my sake, for everyone
Who lives in pain, and yearns for sun,
In Cell Block Twenty-Nine.

Moscow Zoo

by A.M. Juster

We saw the mass grave at the Moscow Zoo.
A sullen man dug up a human skull
Then held it high for journalists to view.
Forensic specialists arrived to cull
Remains and clues from this forgotten plot
On which the zoo still plans to cage a bear.
The experts guessed these prisoners were shot
For special reasons; no one was aware
Of comparable scenes at urban sites.
No one knew if these bones belonged to spies,
Suspected Jews or zealous Trotskyites,
But none of us displayed the least surprise
When bureaucrats emerged from quiet cars
To hint this might have been the work of czars.

Letter to England

for Tommy Robinson

by Joseph Charles MacKenzie

I.

But *yesterday*, your noble fathers bled
Upon the fields of France, where countless dead
Had found among the vines their final rest,
To gild with fame a venerated crest
Whose princely brandishing from age to age
Outlasted armies and the tyrant's rage.
But *yesterday*, you bravely fought and won
A war against the socialistic Hun
Who sought to clap you in the helot's chains
And seize the free world's economic reins.
Again, but *yesterday*, the darkest hour
Of all the world you lifted by your power,
When many owed so much to you, so few,
Across all continents and oceans blue;
No sacrifice too great, no effort spared,
You rallied to the battle and declared,
In England's name, the inauspicious fight
Against the German Marxist and his spite.
When fire from your once-peaceful skies rained down
On London's ancient temples of renown,
Your valor triumphed over every fear
Whose darkness could not mute your English cheer.
You fought, yet weeping for your sons that died,
And rose to glory on your fathers' pride!

II.

Would you, brave sons of Britain's best
Now crawl in servitude at the behest
Of Prussia's despot and her Eastbourne stooge,
And let your nation fall to subterfuge?
Would you embrace their *Novus Ordo* plot
To make you into something you are not,
Abandoning your martyrs' ancient faith
In globalist apostasy to bathe,
Or sanctify Mohammed's violent hordes
Who now seize power from your local lords?
Your government, a servile rubber-stamp,
Now makes your world into a migrant camp.
Already London teems with Saracens,
But will not welcome us Americans!

Full many are the masks that Satan wears:
Take Corbyn and his self-anointing airs,
Nicola Sturgeon and Theresa May,
Who nourish Brussels while your towns decay.
These bear no love for you and never will,
But count as meaningless the nation's will.
For Britain's debt you have these frauds to thank:
What is their "Europe" but a German bank?
Whose fattened bureaucrats, a pampered club,
Appropriate your wealth, your selves to snub!
Corrupt, they steal and loot without surcease:
What Hitler lost through war they grab through peace!
Would you allow their constant plundering
To go unspoken with their blundering?
Surrender speech to their repressive state
To share with the Chinese a eunuch's fate?
Would you let England topple on the brink,
Whilst petty deskmen dictate what you think?
Or let robotic censors gag your cries,
While leftists freely spew their shop-worn lies?

For, Freedom's charter is an empty creed,
Until the day Tom Robinson is freed!

III.

Fair England, land of hills and columbine,
Most gracious land of rills and eglantine,
Return to thy devout, ancestral ways,
The regal virtues of thy former days!
Come forth in splendor, pow'r, and might,
Proclaim thy fealty to truth and right!
Arise, O England, take thy rightful place,
Let not the heathen thy good self debase!
The sun is rising on thy fields of green
And glory waits for thee in stars unseen.
The sword of Arthur has ennobled thee:
Thou wast not made for chains and slavery.
The clang of battle on the winds of time
And shouts of knights that echo in my rhyme,
Resound today in every village square
And rise to heaven like an antique prayer,
That there will always and forever be
An England where the mind and heart are free
To celebrate her once and future King
Whom prophets prophesied and poets sing,
That Mary's Dowry not be spent in vain
But magnify the Holy Virgin's reign,
When Christ shall every bond of hate unbind
And England hold a torch for all mankind.

Tommy Robinson: An Englishman who was tried and imprisoned for reporting on a trial of a sexually predatory gang comprising mostly Pakistani Muslims.

Novus Ordo: Literally "New Order," refers to liberal reforms within the Catholic church that begin in 1965.

Mary's Dowry: Traditional reference to England

122

King Arthur by Charles Ernest Butler, 50 x 30 in., oil on canvas, 1903.

Tbilisi თბილისი

(1976–1978)

by Ralph C. La Rosa

In Soviet Georgia, I feel linguistic shock.
At first assuming residents speak Russian,
I say *Nyet*, not *Ara*, igniting discussion
of Moscow's nagging, Russifying clock
alarms, as predictable as tick and tock.
Zviad says that now the constitution
requires Russian for higher education—
His dissident friends shout *Ara*! *Ara*! and mock.

My heartbeats speed in concert with their rage
fueling widespread rioting. Their nerve
still vital, more than a century in the cage
of Russian rule. *Ara*! They will preserve
the mother tongue—as precious as their blood.
They win this time and plan to win for good.

Russian Nyet: Hem (No)
Georgian Ara: არა *(No)*

*Note: Georgia thwarted two major Moscow efforts in the late 1970s,
and it was the first soviet republic to secede from the USSR. Zviad
Gamsakurdia, the leading dissident and my colleague at Tbilisi State
University, was arrested soon after the riots of April 1977.*

The Cost of Higher Education

by James A. Tweedie

I am a university in the U.S. of A.
Becoming more dependent on Red China every day.
We seek out Chinese students for the money that they bring,
While the Confucius Institutes keep propagandizing.

We bow and scrape to please that country's communist elite,
And neither say nor do what they might feel is indiscreet.
We'll not dispute their sovereign claim on the South China Sea,
Or that Tibet and Taiwan are part of the PRC.

We won't condemn the persecution of the Falun Gong,
Or say that China's foreign policy is right or wrong.
We won't invite the Dalai Lama to a conference
Because the Chinese leadership has said they'll take offense.

When China tears all Christian crosses down, what's there to say?
Instead, we'll condemn Israel and look the other way.
The Tiananmen massacre is a historic fact
Our China Studies program tries to play down or redact.

Pollution and corruption in Beijing we may acknowledge,
Unless it sparks a threat to cut off funding for our college.
All faculty aspiring to travel, live, or teach there
Cannot be China critics if they ever hope to reach there.

For they know China both recruits and hires student spies
To report anything re China they may criticize.
They also know that whether they're emeritus or young,
Their visas will be canceled if they don't control their tongue.

Our campus celebrates free speech, we pamper and adore it.
Unless it hurts our bottom line, in which case we ignore it.
We proudly claim that freedom, truth, and justice are our goal,
But for Red China's money we have sold our very soul.

They Come For One, They Come For All

on the recent and coordinated banning of Alex Jones'
media outlet Infowars.com by Google, YouTube,
Facebook, and Apple (and later, Twitter)

by Seer Ablicadew, BDW

They come for one, they come for all, we see it on our phones.
The media elite is coming after Mr. Jones.
They come for one, they come for all, we see it with our eyes.
They make their backroom deals with dictators and their lies.
The apple bitten in the garden by the goo-twit-face
is smitten with its evil power, going after grace.
They come for one, they come for all, the thought-police of text.
One wonders who they're coming for, and who will be the next.
They come for one, they come for all, if you are reading this,
beware you may be next in line, if they find you amiss.

Venezuelan Woes

by Lud Wes Caribee, BDW

As Socialist experiment Venezuela sinks
into far greater depths, a plunging country on the brink,
Maduro, striving for an orderly recovery,
has pegged the bolivar to petro cryptocurrency.
He has increased the minimum wage sixty-some percent;
the problem is the shops cannot afford to pay their rent.

While beautiful Venezuela sinks into abyss,
upon its current strategy of Socialism's bliss,
where uncooked chickens cost just 14,000,000 bolivars,
and hundred-thousands leave the land on foot. Who can drive cars?
The problem is the other nations do not want their poor;
Peru, Brazil, and Ecuador are closing up their doors.

A New Surveillance Grid

by Esca Webuilder, BDW

Leaked documents show Silicon is plotting to launch forth
a censoring search engine for the Chinese dictaforce;
so government officials can then blacklist thoughts they hate,
like human rights, democracy, religion, truth, and fate.
The Google project codenamed Dragonfly is on the way,
with apps, like Maotai, to keep the populace at bay.
The Firewall of China is not great, nor is it good;
but Google leaders, like Pichai, would like to join its hood;
and that way they can help support suppressing Chinese folk.
Democracy dies in the darkness of an evil yoke.

Dirty Hands

by Connie Phillips

The evil specter's dirty hands
Have soiled the windows to the world.
It's smeared them with the blood and tears
Of millions killed throughout the years.

The evil specter's vicious lies
Have spoiled the children of the world.
It's pierced their brains, destroying faiths
And rendering them hollow wraiths.

The evil specter's crumbling house
Is such an eyesore in the world,
It's harboring a discontent
That shelters hate and ill intent.

Communism's evil ghost
Still lives, and morphs throughout the world.
From socialist to modernist
Mankind's traditions are dismissed.

The evil specter's usurped God
And wants control of all the world.
To lure pure hearts is its desire,
And burn their souls in demon fire.

The evil specter's twisted face
Will be exposed for all the world,
And windows all will be washed clean—
A retribution never seen.

Triumph of the Guillotine by Nicolas-Antoine Taunay, oil on canvas, 50.8 x 66.1 in., circa 1795. This painting depicts the evil of the French Revolution's Reign of Terror. The decapitating execution device used on so many innocent people takes center stage, but the painting reveals that participants are actually in hell. Cannibalism and inhumanity have run amok, and even the demons of hell are fleeing on the left.

The Beast Once Foretold

by Evan Mantyk

The beast once foretold for the end of days
Crouched in a Karl Marx statue erected
Last month in Germany, where it displays
A villain's face now praised and respected.

The beast's scales are the merchandise array,
With Che Guevara, Chairman Mao, red stars,
And sickle-hammer imprints, sold today;
Its horns are tortured lives and grimy bars;

Each pore beneath reads "Made in China," which
Is stamped on every other thing you own,
And make the beast's red color deep and rich;
Fed well on innocent blood, it has grown.

But should we enter further, through its mouth
(The doorway into Lenin's tourist tomb),
A truth about the beast is figured out:
That all the world, it's poised to now consume.

The harmony of classes that each sage
Through history and every nation's past
Sought to preserve with word or pen on page
Has nearly come to breathe its noble last,

While jealousy fills up like abscess pus
And turns each countryman against the next.
Thus, in its jaws, the beast is crushing us;
Equality is just the beast's pretext.

And also pinned within its hungry jaws,
Belief in unseen powers great and good
That stipulate our basic moral laws—
A fact world cultures all once understood.

Without a conscience, we grow cancerous:
Transgender, gay rights, gangs, and drugs, what's next?
Such shameful acts destroy the souls of us;
While freedom is another beast pretext.

Yet, in its heart, the beast fears most of all
Just human beings, we, who have the gall,
We serfs and lords, we sinners low, saints tall,
Who will not let that bastard make us fall!

Sonnet II: Liu Xitong

*Calligrapher Liu Xitong (pronounced Leo She-tong) recently
spoke on Capitol Hill about the persecution he faced in
communist China for his practice of Falun Gong.*

by Evan Mantyk

They strip him down, but cannot strip his soul.
They splash on salty water tasting of
The bitterness of years of state control,
But cannot ruin sweetness from above.

They scrape away the flesh upon his back
And let the salt work stinging misery,
But what they scrape away with their attack
Reveals a flesh that knows no atrophy.

They poke his fingers and his toes with needles,
Pour burning liquid on his genitals
And poison down his throat; such endless evils
Try but fail to make sure goodness stalls.

Though they can stop his hand's calligraphy,
His life has writ in blood: "Set China free."

Subversive Rhyme

by Joe Tessitore

The censor swings her iron fist
and pounds your name into her list
of those whose verse is not in sync
with what their fellow comrades think.

The cultural pronouncements state
that written word must celebrate
our workers and their noble cause;
you may have broken several laws.

Your poetry is at an end!
It might pervert, it might offend!
Yours is the most pernicious crime:
potentially subversive rhyme!

A Baby

by Joe Tessitore

A human egg, a human sperm
What else is there can come to term
But a baby?

Confronted with these simple facts
The wisdom of our time reacts
With a "maybe,"

While souls of babies yet unborn
Who're from their earthly mothers torn
Cry out daily,

And those who hear it can't but cringe
On selfishness's state-funded binge;
They look palely

And summon in their chest a voice
That yells for those who have no choice:
"Hear the baby!"

The Sordid Socialists and Cultish Communists

by Roy E. Peterson

The sordid socialists
and cultish communists
Are really both the same.
They come with greedy fists
Yet give you all the blame.

They blame the rich for working,
For their industry.
They blame the rich while shirking
Their humanity.

They redistribute wealth
Till everyone is poor.
They tax as if our health
Needs taxes more and more.

The pimps of socialism
Buy whores they can control.
Their short-term mechanism
Is handing out a dole.

They hate that things have merit,
Great inventions reign.
They want to know your profit,
Privacy disdain.

The sordid socialists
And cultish communists
Have focused feral eyes
On top of their hit lists:
America's the prize.

V. OBSERVATIONS

Welcome Home by Abraham Hunter, 12 x 16 in
(also 16 x 20 in., in limited edition), acrylic on board, 2015.

How to Plant a Tree

by Alan Sugar

Allow for growth; dig wide—but not too deep.
Add soil amender to the raw red clay.
Remove the rope. Take burlap bag away.
Surround the root ball, mulch, and go to sleep.

And as the roots unfold and slowly creep,
you'll dream of branches long that lean and sway.
And after many years, you'll see—one day,
against the sky, bright leaves that softly sweep.

No matter where you roam, it will remain.
And it will stay and wait for you, alone.
Out there, it will withstand the cold, the rain,
and, in December, winds that cry and moan.
And when you then return, one day, in pain,
you'll find there shade—a shelter and a home.

Kant

by Connor Rosemond

Out of the crooked timber laid by man,
No straight foundation may ever be built.
While Reason clinkers on across the span,
The tunes of Sin jaunt forward with a lilt.
To lie, to steal, to feel in ill no guilt,
To follow Peter's thrice denial there
Before the day of blood through treason spilt;
That is the nat'ral state of man's affairs.

But Reason also leads us off from err,
For through our wit we find morality.
Despite the bent of man toward disrepair,
We can still choose to live in sanctity.

Emotions burked, let this be understood:
There is no better aim than to be good.

Wasteheart

by David Whippman

The precious are so easy to neglect:
I let them down, my family and my friends.
It's futile if I offer my respect—
Today is much too late to make amends.
Nothing is left for me to do or say.
The fact is: my priorities were wrong.
So much affection simply poured away:
I see that now; why did it take so long?
My time, my love: I squandered them, instead
Of using them. It can't be altered now;
most of those I should have loved are dead.
The waste of it all: how could I allow
The waves of my emotions to break and roar
Upon a distant and irrelevant shore?

Philosopher

for Czesław Miłosz

by Leo Yankevich

For a moment as brief and long as eternity
he sees what the blind man sees in the blink of an eye:
a sun that never sets, forms wrought from gold, purity
before it falls or is restored to grace, the gray sky

beheld from the far side of dawn. As if in a dream,
he walks amid universals, essences of names,
and marvels at the beauty of birds, the snowflakes teem-
ing through the ethereal windows of souls, and the flames

of dear dead Heraclitus—now at last understood.
For as long as a moment *is* he sees the Father
embrace the Son—forever since the onset of time.

He has climbed out of the phantasmical cave for good,
martyred by what rills in the blood, no longer bothered
by those in fetters—yet part of the natural crime.

Pika

by André Le Mont Wilson

The pika climbs the snowless slopes in hope
of finding cooler climes. A tailless kin
to hares, he shelters under stones to cope
with rising temps within his furry skin.

The ball of fur appears to roll than hop.
From rock to rock, he gathers summer sedge
and dries his store of winter food atop
a stack of hay to give his life an edge.

At lower elevations, glaciers melt
and won't return. Sierra summers grow.
At higher elevations, showers pelt
this chap. His drooping head awaits the snow.

When climate changes fail to chill the sky,
the sun's increasing heat will kill this guy.

Buzzed by Robert Schlenker, Bigskywildlifeart.com,
11 x 14 in., oil on board.

Wheelbarrows

by Clinton Van Inman

Real love comes not with Cupid's arrows
Nor written on golden leaves;
It comes with picks and wheelbarrows,
With sweat and rolled up sleeves.

Fear

a ballad

by Amy Foreman

I said to Fear, "Away from here!"
And, softly, he withdrew.
But, lost in thought, I plain forgot
To bar the door anew.

So Faith and I sat down to try
And chat the night away.
But while we talked, outside, Fear stalked
And waited for his day.

That time came soon, next afternoon,
Once finished with my work.
I tidied up, sat down to sup,
Then started with a jerk.

From down the hall, an icy Pall
Came creeping to my chair.
He filled the room with horror's gloom
And held me in his snare.

"Oh, Faith," I cried, now terrified,
"Why aren't you here with me?"
But Fear had moved in, unapproved,
And Faith I could not see.

The sun now set, I felt a sweat
So clammy on my skin.
Anxiety came over me,
And panic from within.

Familiar Dread had stopped me dead;
I struggled now to act.
To overcome, to not succumb
To keep my mind intact.

In my despair, I breathed a prayer:
"God, help my unbelief.
Don't leave me now; please don't allow
This evil, wretched Thief,

This eerie Wraith to steal my Faith
To fill this house with fright.
Please fortify my mind so I
Can conquer Fear tonight."

And suddenly, I felt him flee,
That dreadful, clammy Ghost.
As Faith came in where Fear had been
Expelled him from his post.

Unwanted guests are often pests,
Unwanted Fear is worse.
He sneaks around without a sound;
He poisons with his curse.

But now I know to overthrow
His monstrous, grasping plan
By asking aid when I'm afraid
From Heaven's Guardian.

The Things I Have Not Done

by Anthony Wang (high school poet)

I have not been to Medford, nor Milan;
I have not seen a war, nor won the peace;
I've risen to six thousand cloudy dawns
that—not once—promised sun, and storms to cease.
I have not stood to spurn the March of Time;
nor have I dreamed of stories minus loss.
Imposter lands do beckon—paths unwind
as stubborn seas remain, to me, uncrossed.
I have not drowned the snowy streets in ink
that pours from some dark room behind my eyes;
nor have I dwelled in candled inns to drink
the lees, when it was all was left behind.
And yet, I say again, on time I borrow:
"Fear not!—for I shall do it all tomorrow."

Open Heart Surgery

by Steven Shaffer

The best day of your life: a child is born!
Start out happy, but get ready to mourn.
You'll try to keep them from all of life's danger,
"Don't eat that and don't talk to a stranger."
You read them the same ridiculous book,
Or play a game where you talk gobbledygook.
You feed them, house them, replace clothes outgrown,
Buy a Barbie, a car, and a new cell phone.
You persevere through the years of ennui,
Spend your savings on a college degree.
And then comes the day when they will announce,
Everything about you they must renounce.
Your views are too weak, or maybe too strong,
But "whatever"—you're just totally wrong.
You remember what you did all along,
Your list of missteps is perhaps lifelong.
You tried very hard, you know that you did,
To do the best you could do for your kid.
Yet, no one you'll find who's better skilled in,
Ripping your heart out than your own children.

How Can We Know?

a villanelle

by Caroline Bardwell

How can we know where we go when we die;
Pondering signs, looking up at the sky,
Wondering if Someone's hearing my cry?

Which religion is right, which one a lie?
Too much in common to outright deny;
How can we know where we go when we die?

Can things exist I don't see with my eye?
I'm not the only one who's asking why;
Wondering if Someone's hearing my cry.

If my God is real and He reigns on high,
Then life has a purpose that money can't buy.
How can we know where we go when we die?

Do you have the answers? Sorry to pry,
I sit here no matter how hard I try,
Wondering if Someone's hearing my cry.

Questions persist as I let out a sigh,
Searching for answers, yet time passes by,
How can we know where we go when we die;
Wondering if Someone's hearing my cry?

I Love This Life

a rondeau

by Janice Canerdy

I love this life in spite of all
the trying times and every wall
I must tear down to find success,
although sometimes my happiness
is thwarted, slowing to a crawl.

When lofty expectations fall
back to the earth, when I feel small
and uninspired, still I express
I love this life.

When joy is overwhelmed by pall,
I'm always able to recall
good times; then peace dispels duress.
When I'm assured the Lord will bless
with sweetness stronger than the gall,
I love this life.

You Poor, Unfortunate Woman

by Janice Canerdy

Last Monday was a special day for me.
You got that big promotion and the raise!
I pity you, for now your life will be
a rat race through a long, nightmarish maze.

You're doomed to spend that extra salary
on nerve pills and work late six days a week.
While I breeze through my work days trouble-free,
you'll wrestle with a future dark and bleak.

You'll have less time to spend with your new man.
I was engaged to him a year ago.
When suddenly he dumped me, I began
to see he's evil. Soon you too will know!

    The lucky ones like me don't wear a frown.
    We've no romance or wealth to tie us down.

Words

by Janice Canerdy

I've written many poems to declare
my joy to be inhabiting this earth.
I've found my words, if numerous or spare,
inadequate to capture life's full worth.

I chose the sonnet and the triolet,
in hopes that each would help me speak my heart
on love of life with clarity and wit
in phrases neither syrupy nor tart.

When words fell short, I tried the villanelle,
pantoum, and kyrielle to help me say
I love the Lord and those with whom I dwell.
Perhaps words will be adequate someday.

    We must tell God and loved ones how we feel;
    so at the throne of language we must kneel.

From My Pocket

written upon finding that most contemporary poems recommended for Poem in Your Pocket Day do not contain rhyme or meter

by Evan Mantyk

From my pocket came cardstock that
    Had the words below inscribed
In letters golden thoughts emblazoned;
    Hear them now described:

"Poems with rhyming and good timing
    Have a certain charm
That makes the brain a speeding train
    That moves the writing arm.

You may say that they're passé
    And shallow in their scope,
Yet discipline will often win
    Without the help of dope.

Call it common or old-fashioned
    And yet what could be
More profound than how words sound when
    Made in harmony,

Like the brass bell's ringing sound swells
    Sending waves afar
With force not random, but from atoms
    Lined like music bars;

Tin and copper smelted proper
    Makes the metal brass,
For each its protons has strict patterns
    And a constant mass.

Things with order and strong borders
    Leave a lasting mark,
Reverberating, undulating
    Here to ages dark,

From those ages and skin pages
    To antiquity
And forward flying past our dying
    To posterity.

Song that's singing! Gong that's ringing!
    Through the poem with rhyme!
Forever living, ever giving
    Meaning through all time!"

Sonnet III: Richard Sternberg

Mr. Sternberg is an evolutionary biologist who was fired from the Smithsonian after okaying the publishing of a peer-reviewed paper that mentioned intelligent design.

by Evan Mantyk

Between the swirling motifs of the mollusk shell,
And codes of nano-data stored to plan its shape,
He sees intelligence that from a mind would swell
And truths that Darwin's startless story can't escape.

Without escape, the scientists instead attacked
By using politics infused with Marx's specter
Against the clearer thinker, who was quickly sacked
And wrongly labeled a religious benefactor.

Within the path that tries reducing organisms
To lower, dead, component parts and nothing more,
A science unafraid that complex mechanisms
Show signs of complex thought, gets slapped down to the floor.

How does from almost nothing grow those splendid shells?
Look up, not down! In other planes the answer dwells.

The Threads

on the state of poetry today

by Evan Mantyk

I see the threads have all aligned
   In a patchwork tapestry
That seemed at first all but resigned
   To the death of poetry.

The colors of the patchwork poems,
   Splendid though each of them seems,
Are mismatched swaths cut off from homes,
   Fraying fast at shoddy seams.

A patch shows stream of consciousness
   (Barely can I read this one).
Another stitched vacuousness
   Boldly, yet without rhyme's fun.

And all of them go their own way,
   Self-expressing endlessly
Unmeasured words in grim array,
   Wove in patterns tastelessly.

Yet from this mess I can make out
   Golden threads as thin as air,
More potent than what is about,
   Grossly scattered everywhere.

These threads are straight, invincible,
   Tempered over times gone by.
Their discipline's immutable,
   Colored in tradition's dye.

They move at once, each with a force
  Greater than this age has known,
And put the tapestry on course
  For an image to be sewn

That brings together every piece
  Willing to be brought in line,
And bunches them into a crease
  Firmly held in hands divine.

That's what I see as threads align
  In a patchwork tapestry
That seems to show a grand design
  For the rise of poetry.

"Write On!" The Masters from the Shadows Cried

by Ted Hayes

"Write on!" the Masters from the shadows cried.
"By your thin air we breathe, nor ever died.
Your modest dress, our glorious raiment shares
And witness to our sun your candle bears.

"Ignored, reviled, by fashion shut away,
We are not stilled, nor sleep as common clay.
We are the living, the unsurpassèd height.
What hand shall drag us down to mortal night?

"A hundred years, and now—the heart's decease;
Ride then, the wind which flies to art's increase,
Our rhyming updrafts, wild currents to the sun—
And in our matchless light, your work be done!"

The Book of Kells

by Jane Blanchard

The intricacies of script and figure are
amazing. Kudos to the faithful who
made contributions large or small. By far
this volume is the greatest ever to
present illuminated gospel. Ink
was carefully applied to skins of calves
bred for this very purpose. Just to think
of such devotion—nothing done by halves—
puts me to shame. As one who tries to craft
a poem now and then for reasons not
exclusively religious, I know—draft
by draft—when I am falling short. No jot
of mine will ever match the artistry
of monks renowned for anonymity.

Shattered Prospects

by David Watt

Pursued by every shadow,
He rode the winding way
To where his love lay waiting:
Trunk packed for ocean stay.

An owl looked on in silence;
A wombat backed away—
It seemed, no-one had noticed
The saddlebag's low sway.

He wore a conscience heavy;
More weighty than the gold
Removed beneath the noses
Of troopers bullet-holed.

But one thought kept him going,
Both resolute and bold—
A dream of life together,
In love as they grew old.

She saw his coattail flapping,
Each vaporous breath rise forth,
The bulging bars of bullion
Purloined from further north.

Then suddenly, from cover,
A bullet followed course;
Resulting in her lover's
Departure from his horse.

She burnt their steamer tickets
Upon the fireplace grate
Until they soon resembled
Her lover's ashen state.

And now, when night comes calling,
Her wistful eyes relate
The power of a gunshot
To shatter prospects great.

A Cello Knows

by Andrew Todd Ramirez

Amidst the smoke and light and laughter,
Along the smiles and cheers thereafter,

A sound is bled, wrung free from strings.
It bounds and treads and wholly sings
Inside each song, a secret's moved,
Not right nor wrong or frequent proved.
The message dances from bow to ear;
A coded trance of love and fear
From left to right the story rings
Of Death and light the Cello brings.
The covert tale engulfs the room
It vibrates truth to those who loom.
The Cello knows for why it's played
Its secret lost, both gone and stayed.

In the smoke and light and laughter,
Music lies and cries thereafter.

An Atheist's Faith

by Ron L. Hodges

If I had the faith of an atheist,
I'd never succumb to my mortal lust.
I could cast mighty mountains out to sea,
Walk across water as those insects ski,
And break the darkness like a brittle crust.

For to believe chance made all this, one must
Hold a steeled mind, shaped and cured not to rust.
Oh, my stumbling soul would have found the key
If I had the faith of an atheist!

No, our universe seems more than pooled dust:
We see such signs of design. To then trust
Constructive destruction brought it to be
Shows such zeal—such raw devotion—to me.
Oh, from nothing could the wonders consist
If I had the faith of an atheist!

A Poem's Purpose

by Michael Maibach

A poet writes
His heart that day,
It is for him
A way to pray.

The reader finds
Those words as new—
Their life unique,
Their story true.

What the poet felt
It matters not,
The reader's task
Is to loose the knot.

To loose the knot
That's closed their heart,
The poem may serve
As their fresh start.

As you read a poem
Ask one thing—
Who might you love?
What bell to ring?

An Allegory of Poetry by Auger Lucas, 23.1 x 21 in.,
oil on panel, 18th century.

Heritage

by Sally Cook

I like to say I'd an Egyptian father
If that is too obscure for you, I'd rather
Explain it just by citing preservation.
They preserved mummies, he his indignation
At how the world had gone awry, once all
Ethics, society had gone on stall.
My father then stepped gingerly among
Past trophies that his ancestors had won.
Hoping his prayer and reverence sufficed

He kept his world on track, but when it iced
Outside, you could not see the dated rocks
He placed beneath his trees and hollyhocks,
Each one a past indignity he buried
Within his boundaries. Although he was harried
By slings of life interred within his yard.
At least he had contained them. It was hard
For him, to live without what used to be—
His venue, and then have to deal with me.

November

by Avery Miller

Of light and warmth and growing things, alas, there's nothing left,
November finds me at my window staring all bereft,
Her puddled eyes and chestnut dress are streaming, shower tossed,
She taps upon my window calling, "Sorry for your loss!"

"But if you are the mother here, there's something you must do,
The children coming in from play are soaking through and through,
They tend to wither, children, just like flowers in the gloom,
The sun can't stay, but he has asked that you light up the room."

Though willing, I'm uncertain; still, it helps to turn on lights,
It's true, we all feel better when the kitchen's warm and bright,
"November, I have found a way to cheer the wilting crew,
With cookies and a fragrant anti-melancholy stew."

"Just so," replies the gray-eyed fairy damsel of the rain,
"A little loving work will cure the blueness in the brain."

The Composition Teacher
Addresses His Class

by Joseph S. Salemi

When naming things, you have to use a *noun*;
A *verb* shows action or a state of being.
An *adjective* describes—that is, marks down
The qualities of objects that you're seeing.

An *adverb* tells you how, or else how soon
A deed is done—say, "painfully" or "fast."
When placed with adjectives they help fine-tune
Descriptive force, like "absolutely gassed."

A *pronoun* takes the place of proper names
Or else alludes to antecedent things.
A *preposition* points, and always frames
The noun or noun-linked phrase to which it clings.

A *participle* emanates from verbs
And functions as a hybrid in good diction.
It can take past or present form, and serves
To add a tense-based nuance to depiction.

Conjunctions tie together words and clauses;
They also can disjoin by act of scission.
Like plus and minus signs, they marshal forces
For union, separation, or division.

An *article* is just an honorific
You put before some nouns so we'll discern
Whether your focus on them is specific
Or just a passing glance of unconcern.

An *interjection* is a mere effusion—
A word you blurt out from your guts or heart
In rage, joy, spite, emotional confusion…
It stands alone, syntactically apart.

These are the parts of speech that make up discourse,
At least for folks in literacy's fold.
So if you're hoping to get by in this course
Don't give me any backtalk—*learn them cold.*

Decay of the Literary Sense

from A Gallery of Ethopaths

by Joseph S. Salemi

For those of us who cherish text,
There's anguish in what I'll say next.
The world of letters, by tradition,
Was one of grace, style, erudition—
A shrine to language at its best,
A temple of the precious blest
Who had achieved the very heights
Of glory in their verbal flights.
All that's gone, like faded dreams;
There's no one left today who seems
To give a damn for perfect craft.
Professors now are dull and daft
Impostors who refuse to judge
Between fine work and worthless sludge.
If you rate books by wit and style
It's sure to rouse your colleagues' bile;
They'll fret and grow antagonistic,
Say your approach is "belletristic,"
And hence not suited to a college
Which deals in abstract lit-crit's knowledge.
If you read books and love them madly
Professors take that very badly.
They say it's quaint and amateurish
And to persist in it is boorish.

Professionals just use the text
To mirror theory, which reflects
All that you need to know when reading—
Love for great works shows lack of breeding
And it's discouraged as a rule
In those who go to graduate school.
As a result, our English teachers
Display these most debased of features:
They have no sense of skill and wit,
Consider all aesthetics shit,
Take no delight in humane letters
And can't tell bad stuff from the better.
Artistic worth takes second place
To gender, class, religion, race,
Or what the faculty define
As the current Party Line.
Writers are judged by whether they
Had something "positive" to say
Advancing a leftish, liberal cause—
Those who did not get scant applause.
Authors are ranked, not by real merit,
But what the prof can find and ferret
Out about how they were enlightened,
Whether their consciousness was heightened,
Whether they're Tory or progressive,
Stolidly bourgeois, or transgressive,
Whether they worked for women's rights
Or raised their voice against social blights.
Writers whose work can pass this muster
Have reputations with new lustre.
Others are judged to be deficient—
Their "social sense" was insufficient,
Or they endure receptions icy
Because their politics were dicey.

Pound, Eliot, and Butler Yeats
(By all sane standards, solid greats)
Are only taught with cautious warning
Laced with prim, high-minded scorning
Because these men all said or wrote
Things that get a liberal's goat.
Some others are in quarantine
Like Byron, Kipling, Scott, Céline—
Most academics can't endure
Their viewpoints, which they deem "impure."
Professors drop these real achievers
For worthless, third-rate, trendy screevers
Who now, because of sex and color,
Are hailed as "major," though they're duller
Than gray paint peeled off wooden pilings,
And all alike as iron filings.
You can dismiss, without ado,
Bell Hooks, Maya Angelou,
Jamaica Kincaid, Audre Lorde,
And all the others in the horde
Of hyped-up, bogus reputations.
They are just media creations
Designed to tip the canon's scales
Against the hated dead white males.
The literary sense has died
And we're left with the putrefied
Golems from miasmic mists
Who fill up college reading lists.

The Stone of the Unknown, West Point Cemetery

by Joe Tessitore

Ye Grave,

Your word confronts me with a start
and makes its way into my heart
inscribes itself and will not leave
so for this one I too now grieve

who gave his life and even more
is there a soul that can ignore
unknown whose fame will surely last
above, beyond, and unsurpassed

unknown for whom our flags unfurl
unknown for whom the bagpipes skirl
unknown but by no means forgot
this hero, all that I am not…

…unspoken but forever heard
can more be said in just one word?

Ms. Hayden, On Your Selection of Our Next Poet Laureate

addressed to the U.S. Librarian of Congress,
Carla Hayden, who selects the U.S. Poet Laureate

by Joe Tessitore

For poetry to rise again
Seek one who has applied the pen
To that which all can understand,
To verse which is sublime and grand.

Choose one who writes for all to read,
Who is from all pretension freed,
Who can be subtle and be bold,
Whose message speaks to young and old.

Seek one whose words can cross the aisle
And turn a scowl into a smile;
Whose elegance is pure and plain
And can be heard in each refrain.

Turn not away from poetry
That can uplift and set us free!

Birth Pangs

by Rohini Sunderam

The painful birth of motherhood
So few have really understood,
Is but a shadow that foretells
The pain our parents knew so well
Of children singing out farewell.

As to their freedom they rush out
With a merry, happy shout:
"See you, mom, papa," they call
Do they look back? Not at all,
Headlong, heeding freedom's call.

While we stay behind, pretend
It's a new beginning, not an end
They have crossed a Finish Line
For the first time, we're left behind
Watching, waiting, marking time.

And these pains unlike birth pangs go
Not in waves, but slow, real slow.
The first sharp stabs are weeks apart;
When they forget to call, your heart
Then feels a spasm really sharp.

They carry on their merry way.
We check our e-mails every day;
Every text on our mobile
Is opened with expectant smile;
Every call is answered while

For them, it's "Can you call back please?"
Rattled off with smiles, with ease
While we hold back our tears today
Say, "Sure, but don't forget, okay?"
And hold off for another day.

Until at last the birth pangs ease;
They never really ever cease.
A day then dawns, they have their own
And that's when you will know they've grown
Their love for you is then full-blown.

It's time for you to smile again;
It's time to let go of the pain;
It's time for them to say to you
Those words of love, born fresh, anew,
"Dear ma, dear pa, we love you too."

Little Girl

by Martin John King

She's fishing in a rock pool
just abandoned by the sea
She's too engrossed within her world
to notice you and me.

She sprawls to draw a picture
open book upon the sand
Great masters never wielded
so delicate a hand.

Her rainbow spreads across the page
to seek a pot of gold
Our little girl within her world
thinks never to grow old.

Bristlecone Longevity

by Phillip Whidden

The beauty of the tree is not how old,
Indeed how ancient in its gnarling now,
Not in its silent history yet untold,
Nor in the pre-historic roots and bough—
Their age—but in its newness ever new,
Its torqued refusal to be caught by death,
Rejection of defeat enclasped in screw-
Shaped trunk, five-thousand-year eon's breath
There in its arid air, determined bark,
Those needles prickly and the feisty cones
Which stand against, aghast, against the stark
Realities which beat against its bones,
    These needles and these cones forever young,
    Which sing forever like a new-made tongue.

Bristlecone: These pine trees are considered among the longest-living life forms on earth. The oldest is dated as being 5,000 years old.

Ars Poetica

"The word 'classic' itself ... derives from the Latin word
classicus which referred to recruits of the 'first class', the heavy
infantry in the Roman army. The 'classical', then, is 'first
class', though it is no longer heavily armoured."
> —*Robin Lane Fox,* The Classical World: An
> Epic History from Homer to Hadrian

by Phillip Whidden

The finest do not win the war with weight
Of numbers. Heavy popularity
Is not enough to stop them. You can freight
The arts with freedoms of vulgarity,
Simplicity, and banging rhymes in verse,
Or wildest sloshes meant to shock the eye
In paintings. You can conjure even worse
In license in a film with all awry
With tastelessness and dirt. There is a way
Which always has been there to make the best
Of creativity. It is the sway
Of formal rules to help the artist wrest
   The power of lawlessness by might of mind
    And make of grossest chaos things refined.

Exultation by Anna Rose Bain, 30 x 20 in, oil on linen, 2014.

Devotion by Anna Rose Bain, 30 x 20 in., oil on linen, 2014.

Heritage as Hope

by Phillip Whidden

I saw the cricket scene in evening light,
In Windsor light with calm men moving through
The evening air and dressed in cricket white.
Long centuries are contained beneath the blue
Of evening sky which folds the chestnut blooms
In its embrace as two teams play by rules
No sky could ever dream. These men are grooms
Of royalty we call tradition. Pools
Of beauty are these matches set in green
And white and blue. They tilt—the future, too
Should England last as long as glories seen
Should linger, glories that are rigid, true.
    When we who live have gone to other bounds,
      Let there be chestnuts still—and cricket grounds.

Exodos, Prologos

to the Class of 2018

by Benjamin Daniel Lukey

In times uncertain, ask your truest friends
For counsel, and take all they say to heart—
But know that we are bound for different ends,
And none but you can learn and play your part.
Some friend may say, "To thine own self be true,"
But "thine own self" is not a thing of stone.
And who can say what time will do to you?
Reflect, and you will see how you have grown
And changed, from year to year and day to day,
In ways, perhaps, that only you can see;
We've gathered here to send you on your way,
And only you can say what that will be.
Be hungry for whatever lies in store,
And make it greater than what came before.

Alzheimer's Disease

by Sam Gilliland

I can feel your deep darkness closing in,
With its harrowing sense of helplessness,
Soon obscenity sours tongues gathering;
Havoc's wrought by every hellish djin
As chaos kicks aside your selflessness,
Guilt, aplenty, glee guilds in fathering:
Flaunting tones of stricken folk fail true faith,
Whilst naught stands twixt birth and eternity;
All is lost to those fondling piety,
Murmuring minds of men lull, so Simon saith,
Womankind mocks mankind's fraternity,
Yet each painful breath plumes anxiety.

No New Jerusalem here, not inside,
Only the Dead may feel self-satisfied.

Poetry Today

by Peter Hartley

If elevated thought had ever been
The least criterion of excellence
In poetry, why should it then be seen
Today as simply of no consequence?
If rhyme was good enough for Shakespeare's time
And rhythm beats in Keats and Chaucer, Blake
And Dryden why then, why is rhyme a crime
And rhythm a mistake for heaven's sake?

Free verse, a curse at worst, its mastery
A hash of slapdash balderdash and bull,
Such tripe the tritest poetastery
Disposed in random rows is just as dull.
Who knows why those to metric rhyme averse
Compose such awful prose and call it verse.

A Fire Extinguisher

by Peter Hartley

Though technical accomplishment held sway
For centuries, some artists of today
Will doubtless scorn such talent as passé.
Once art stood on its merits and would say
My worth resides in what you see in me,
Not what your facile pseudo-intellect
Extrapolates from what you think you see,
Confected with the guff we all expect.

Collectors, artists, critics must have all
Conspired in symbiosis to inspire
Tate Modern's latest coup: upon the wall
Its finest purchase yet, a smart new fire
Extinguisher. Just think of all that hype
It garnered, hanging there among the tripe.

A Picture of a Horse

by Peter Hartley

While at a gallery one day appears
A little mob of children, come to see
Some Pollock drips, a few of Rothko's smears,
And several of Picasso's ears set free
To roam about the same side of his face.
Their teacher showed a painting of a horse.
"And that's supposed to be a horse, in case
You can't read what the label says of course,"

She said, and then a little boy piped "So
Why isn't it a horse?" and she was at
A loss. It looked more like a portmanteau,
A set of bagpipes or a stovepipe hat,
But gave one the impression of a horse.
Why wasn't it a picture of a horse?

Oak

by Jeffrey Essmann

In quiet awe before a solid oak
in summer bloom, I thought: to such as these
my Saxon kin of long ago bespoke
their pagan prayers—a source of great unease
to Charlemagne, these heathens and their trees!
He killed all those beyond baptism's hope,
Then celebrated Christmas with the pope.

And longer yet ago the priests of Zeus
the rustling tones of oak leaves would attend,
thereby the god's good pleasure to deduce
and by their oracles his voice extend,
that men their earthly ways might wisely wend.
Odysseus they hurried back to Greece
the suitors of his wife there to police.

My priesthood, though, seems a shabbier thing
as a wind from Jersey rustles the leaves
and Bronxward breathes. Yet time can sing
when summer sunlight coolly ebbs and heaves
and mottled shadows pool and interweave.
Then Zeus just mumbles "beauty…" in my ear—
some days, the only oracle I hear.

The Afternoon of Man

by Jeffrey Essmann

Fourteen or so, one autumn afternoon,
my homework done and supper hours away,
I scuffed along on sodden paths bestrewn
with yellowed leaves in woods where I'd once played.
Perhaps it was the setting sun that grayed
the air, perhaps a sudden chill just then,
but something in my soul began to weigh
the thought I'd never be a boy again.
And now as I move through the world of men,
live by my wits and somewhat by my strength,
there nonetheless still comes the time at length,
late afternoon inside my office when
I of a sudden catch the subtle musk:
the sour smell of oak leaves in the dusk.

A Single Blade of Grass

by Michael Curtis

A single blade of grass can make
 A thousand miles green;
A twig a mighty stone can break—
 This I myself have seen.

What more the seed that holds the life
 That cannot be denied:
The will of God who sparks the light
 That all things hold inside.

Can steel in time the pattern break,
 Can we unchain the soul,
Can feeble minds their walls forsake,
 Will atoms let us go?

These cities raised on high by hand
 By seeds will crumble down,
And everything of man will fall
 When nature claims her own.

Thought

by Michael Curtis

Drop a stone within a word,
  No bottom will you find,
No distant splash will be heard
  In the depths of mind.

The waves upon the ocean's top
  Betray its rocky floor;
Though deep and broad its edges stop,
  A thought breaks on no shore.

The distant stars no eye can see,
  Nor time, a clock define,
Yet even these eternities
  Are sand specks in the mind.

Broader than the lap of God
  Wherein all glory fits,
Thought, forever bottomless,
  Devours all that exists.

Tiger Fire

by Sally Sandler

The fire waits with tiger paws
on silent haunches by the hill,
then mounts the rock with clinging claws,
and contemplates the moment it will

pounce—on sagebrush dry as bones,
under a ghostly quiet moon,
slink through tinder, stalking homes,
and spring atop a shingled roof.

In blazing orange-black-white cape
it roars at scorching desert sky,
dives on prey, devours the take,
smoldering embers in its eye.

We scan the canyons, fear the sight
of fire—the tiger in the night.

Be Free

by Connie Phillips

"I need," "I want," "I wish"… desire—
The hunger burns inside, like fire.
To profit, gain, amass, acquire:
This seems to be all we require.

God gives us each just what we need
To live the life we're meant to lead—
No competition, sans the greed.
If we have faith, we can succeed.

Have patience, kindness, honesty,
And give to others lovingly.
Compassion truly is life's key:
Unlock your heart, and you'll be free.

Rushing

by Alexander King Ream

There is no right way to work what is wrong,
Rushing the shui and missing the feng.

Turning, Burning, Churning

by Alexander King Ream

In a dream, I turned from sin,
Resolving not to fail again,
And in my dream I saw the myth
In all its real and churning pith.

Above the dream there spun a wheel
And burned an engine wrought of steel;
Though right, it wrenched from wrong and ill,
And sight and stench were awful, still.

For Food I Could Never Find

Breathe forth your words now, breaking at long last
The fasting that has kept me hungering
For food that I could never find on earth.
　　　—*Dante Alighieri*, The Divine Comedy,
　　　　　　　　　　Paradiso xix.25-27

by James Sale

For food I could never find
How long I fasted I can't say;
Always a fullness on my mind
Bid me hasten on my way.

For food I could never find:
How hunger drove me night and day;
Always somehow made mad my mind.
I'd want to stop but couldn't stay.

For food I could never find.
How seeming good but tasting clay;
Always voracious in my mind,
I'd start to focus then would stray.

For food I could never find:
How meat at first turned quick to hay;
Always projecting in my mind
I'd start with yes but come to nay.

For food I could never find:
How long for heaven I would pray;
Always the manna, thin as wind,
Evaporated on my tray.

For food I could never find
And if I could, could never pay;
Always that debt was on my mind,
Always in eating more delay.

For food I could never find.

Canto I

by James Sale

It had to be—that long descent began:
About me images, one century
That started, stuttered, showed how poor is man

In all things except his savagery.
My grandfather's face, first in that stale line,
Who missed the trenches through admin's mystery;

Was sent instead to fight in Palestine,
While friends he'd known all died in No-Man's-Land.
How lucky, then, for him; for me a sign:

Despite the misery, unintended, unplanned
That characterized the fools who sought to build
A better world—progress—to make a stand,

As it were; as if politics could field
A force sufficient to overcome gods
Whose power, agencies were not like to yield

To mortal die, its throes and sadder odds.
Or, as if science, too, could weight outcomes—
Build Babels better far than Nimrod did.

Yet for all that building, they built one tomb
Called planet Earth—polluted, warmed, and dying,
Neglecting the while to study, exhume

The corpse of what the century was frying.
That long descent began. I saw myself as heir;
I saw myself for poetry is scrying—

Calliope come to me now, be here,
For I must tell how I came to that wild place
Where death is our doctrine, and twin despair.

Canto 1: Dante in the Wilderness by Eric Armusik,
48 x 60 in., oil on AlumaComp aluminum panel, 2017.

For all this, know—each human hides that face
Divine, which is our task, within our will,
To reveal at last, if so by God's grace,

That Love that Dante saw created hell,
And by His goodness covered Earth with stars,
So many, no mind could count them, they fill

The cosmos, yet hang so near us, yet far;
Our destiny, one day, perhaps, to cross
Over to where mortality can't mar,

Cast shadows, that prolong and deepen loss.
Calliope come now to me, epic queen:
Without inspiration, writing is dross;

Enable me to see what's not been seen
Before, but rise heroic to this quest
And find the Grail: what does this century mean?

And in so doing also find true rest—
The ninth heaven where Dante found himself,
Surprised and speechless, all light and all blest,

All one, yet being not somebody else:
Himself full-on, even as one snowflake
In dawn's deep drift, unique whilst still engulfed.

Calliope, Apollo's daughter, make
Me prophesy: you know what's to be,
You know the golden god and how he breaks

The proud. I came myself near history,
Despite a false summer then broken out,
Collapsing quite incomprehensibly.

Something medics came to see in my gut,
Something small, some shadow, should not be there,
But they'd remove—a snip—at most a cut

And I'd be well; there my life would be clear.
I waited hospitalized without sun,
No moon either, nothing natural, dear—

Gone without trace, as I went down, down, down:
One held my hand as anesthetics did
Their graft—what was to do would soon be done;

And that malignancy within, well hid,
That choked, snake-like, intestinal flesh,
Would be revealed at last and I'd be rid

Of cancer's bloated presence and its wish:
Destruction absolute, assured, aligned—
Refusing life, wanting in death to mesh

With me, an apt image of evil's mind,
Small gains to build one vaulting emptiness,
At last undo what so much love designed.

What much love designed? And too was blessed?
Such sacredness I scarce can speak of—how
Before God now I tremble, quake, am less—

His glory. I saw it, as dying, slow,
Gutted of guts and lying on the bed,
Out of my body, sight soared to space, so

Effortlessly, and there I saw, ahead,
One giant finger turning candyfloss.
Wondering what—? I willed myself and sped

To see. There, close-up, I saw not chaos,
But its just opposite: not sugar wound
Around a finger, for which some child might fuss,

But a star formed in deep space, without sound,
No fanfare, tranquil; and the index bent,
One flick, it reveled forward on its round.

How could such power be—the whole cosmos rent
Into parts and each part on its own work,
And better still, each atom purposeful, sent

Whilst far below on a bed, injured, hurt,
Powerless to do evil, much less good,
I lay helpless, fit soon to be but dirt?

I choked, for knowing there's nothing I could
Do, racked on my bed of pity, undone,
Undoable. "Lord, God!" My tears a flood

That nothing conscious might make or sum:
Only a baby in the night in pain
Hopes somehow something or someone must come

Because existence exists and—come again?—
Not only did He make the living ones,
He's Life itself, which means ... He is the plan.

I cried, "Lord God, help me!"—and just the once—
Just as the finger turned, leisurely, out
Toward the void where all other stars shone,

And it seemed that He—the same He no doubt
Disturbs or interrupts—that that One might
Leave me forever stuck in my dark rut

Despairing, with those who mock without right,
Just then, before my thought caught my words' sense,
He turned, unflexed, had me direct in sight

Before I could marshal the least defense
Even, discern my spirit from my soul,
Before I knew even my existence,

So fast, so instant, light itself seemed slow:
There, at the point the surgeon made his cut,
At that point exactly I felt God's blow

In me—so in me that nothing could stop
Its force, its flow, and in one instant all changed,
As if mortality itself were shut

Off, and for it something brand new exchanged:
I mean that pain, in body and mind, ceased,
As suffering, past and present, was expunged,

And paradise abounded, total peace,
And more: His face I could not see, but rather
His presence, working within, me released.

But that was it—free—yet in me, together,
And I aware of some awful purity:
A whiteness of light, which recalling ever

I quake within, tremble before to Be,
Before such beauty as I cannot stand
Before. So weeping, weeping endlessly,

Not tears as lost souls weep, you understand,
But joy at such happiness—profound, deep,
So deep nothing could undo, countermand,

Erase. At last my soul was in His keep—
And so He rocked me like a babe in arms,
The only time in three months I found sleep.

Nothing could interrupt that restorative calm:
No artificial light, blood tests, chit-chat
Or worse, the dying cries lacking love's balm

In that hell of a hospital I was at,
Broke that deep sleep that God induced in me;
Till morning, sunlight at the window slats,

Waking to find, or know for certainty,
I was not bound to die, but yet to live,
For He had called me back, through His mercy,

All grace, unbounded, simply His to give.
The world strange, which not long before was not—
Altered; before, the busy bustling hive

Of bees circling till, exhausted and shot,
They died in beds of blank indifference;
After, honey and overflow, the lot—

Time slowed to tripartite significance,
Future ahead, and present, a new past
In which what was random had His Presence,

Vital, pervading all moments, all mass,
Nothing beyond reaching beyond His reach,
That reach, and His hand, the net He had cast.

That net into which He too had been pitched.
No, not some distant god who lived remote,
Pulling the levers and strings, laughing as each

Man fell to common and singular notes
Of folly: no, not such a god as that,
Or some such Zeus on full sensual bloat,

Careless how the swan's neck proves Troy's mishap;
Instead, another God, and just the One,
Whose Word upholds all things, all changing shapes,

Till changing He Himself in flesh was done;
And now before me changes what's ahead
Beckons, a door, burning to drape upon

As if hanging, and hanging there my bed—
Out to deeper depths than this sick ward holds
And sinking at last the human cancer shed

If seeing my own horror and its toll
Might let light intrude, penetrate my soul.

VI. TRANSLATIONS

Montalvo Bacchante by Clark Gussin, 30 x 24 in., charcoal drawing, 2016.

Angels

by Rainer Maria Rilke (1875–1926)
from German by Leo Yankevich

They all have mouths that tire,
bright souls that have no seams.
And longing (for sin's mire)
passes through their dreams.

Almost alike they stride,
silent beneath the Tree,
like intervals inside
great God's grand symphony.

But when one of them rages,
spread wings set tempests spinning,
as if God, sculpting ages,
huge-handed, leafed through pages,
the dark book of beginning.

Die Engel

Sie haben alle müde Münde
und helle Seelen ohne Saum.
Und eine Sehnsucht (wie nach Sünde)
geht ihnen manchmal durch den Traum.

Fast gleichen sie einander alle;
in Gottes Gärten schweigen sie,
wie viele, viele Intervalle
in seiner Macht und Melodie.

Nur wenn sie ihre Flügel breiten,
sind sie die Wecker eines Winds:
als ginge Gott mit seinen weiten
Bildhauerhänden durch die Seiten
im dunklen Buch des Anbeginns.

The Lord's Supper

by Rainer Maria Rilke (1875–1926),
from German by Leo Yankevich

They're gathered round, astonished, full of dread,
round him who like a wise man must decide,
and who leaves those with whom he's broken bread,
and who comes like a stranger from outside.
Old solitude haunts him, Gethsemane,
though once it bound him to astounding acts;
now he will walk through every olive tree,
and those who love him turn away their backs.

He's called them to the table, past the stoves,
and (like birds woken by shots from the groves)
he humbles their hands from among the loaves
with his own words: and toward him they fly,
flawed, fluttering; and yet with all their power,
they look for ways out, since the time is nigh,
but he is everywhere, like twilight hour.

Das Abendmahl

Sie sind versammelt, staunende Verstörte,
um ihn, der wie ein Weiser sich beschließt,
und der sich fortnimmt, denen er gehörte,
und der an ihnen fremd vorüberfließt.
Die alte Einsamkeit kommt über ihn,
die ihn erzog zu seinem tiefen Handeln;
nun wird er wieder durch den Ölwald wandeln,
und die ihn lieben, werden vor ihm fliehn.

Er hat sie zu dem letzten Tisch entboten
und (wie ein Schuß die Vögel aus den Schoten
scheucht) scheucht er ihre Hände aus den Broten
mit seinem Wort: sie fliegen zu ihm her;
sie flattern bange durch die Tafelrunde
und suchen einen Ausgang. Aber er
ist überall wie eine Dämmerstunde.

The Explosion

by Ryhor Krushyna (1907–1979),
from Belarusian by Ihar Kazak

May mayhem never strike our good Earth;
The fertile one deserves tranquility and gratitude,
So that on earth where in ruins weeds give birth,
There would be no malevolent attitude.

>   But evil—
>   an explosion…
>   Again
>   a *wormwood*
>   spill.

Fear… What abyss for our populous world's race!
Indeed, fatal is this abyss!
Humanity—it seems to them—has conquered space!
But the enraged atom is on its throne and much amiss.

>   But evil—
>   an explosion…
>   Again
>   a *wormwood*
>   spill.

Wormwood: anything bitter or grievous (Webster); in Belarusian it is known as byl'nik or byl'nyog, the chernobyl' plant—a prophetic statement since it was written in the mid-1960s before the Chernobyl ear disaster.

ВЫБУХ

Хай ня будзе бязладзьдзя на добрай зямлі:
Пладаноснай—спакой у падзяку,
Каб на ёй, дзе руіны травой параслі,
Ня было-б аніякага знаку.
    А злыбедай—
    выбух…
    Ізноў
    быльнёг
    выбег.

Страх, якое прадоньне на люднай зямлі!
Так, фатальнае тое прадоньне!
Людскі космас—здаецца ім—перамаглі,
А разьюшаны атам—на троне.
    А злыбедай—
    выбух…
    Ізноў
    быльнёг
    выбег.

Springtime in Autumn

by Ryhor Krushyna (1907–1979),
from Belarusian by Ihar Kazak

On bushes the cobwebs are settling,
And yellowed leaves are falling.

Armillaria mushrooms hug tree-stumps along the way—
They're delegates of a commencing autumn day.

Though my age is now at a gray stage,
Spring is sprouting forth from my pen upon each page.

I write with more of a fiery sense
To find an unquenchable love without pretense.

In order to find it among mankind,
So that hatred would not make us so blind.

May spring blossom forth for me in fall,
And sing out with full compassion's call.

Now fully tuned is my mood
And my former complaints are spewed.

I gaze onto the young forest of pines,
There I see spring's verdant signs.

Вясна Ўвосень

Села павуціньне на кусты,
Падаюць пажоўклыя лісты.

Туляцца апенькі каля пня—
Дэлегаты восеньскага дня.

Хоць са мной сьсівелая пара,
А вясна сьпявае з-пад пяра,

Я пішу ў запальным пачуцьці,
Каб любоў нясгасную знайсьці,

Каб яе знайсьці сярод людзей,
Каб нянавісьць гойсала радзей.

Мне вясна ўвосень хай цьвіце,
І пяе ў шырокай дабраце.

У мяне наструнены настрой
І няма бурклівасьці старой.

Заглядаю ў хвойнік малады,
Там вясны хялёныя сьляды.

Longing

by Friedrich Schiller (1759–1805),
from German by David B. Gosselin

If I from this darkened valley
Where the gloomy vapors creep
Might by some wonder swiftly flee
My soul could blessedly weep!
Gazing upon these pure serene
Eternal hills through heaven fare,
Had I wings to climb this scene
My spirit would scale the air.

I hear those melodious strains
Descending in soothing streams,
While the restoring breeze and rains
Carry the heavens' sweet dreams;
Luscious fruit there ripening hangs
On never-wilting branches
Flowers there don't fear the fangs
Of the winter's ravishes.

Oh! How sweet it must be to dwell
Under the eternal sun
How the sanguine airs must softly blow
Through the woods so frolicsome.
But the foaming waters stifle
My frail attempts at crossing
And my frightened soul can but toil
Before those torrents frothing.

See! A lonely bark is rocking
And it seems no helmsman's there,
Sails are open, waves are foaming,
But should a mortal soul dare?
Then its courage and faith alone
Must direct it—not God's hand;
Only magic carries a man
To that magic wonderland.

Sehnsucht

Ach, dieses Thales Gründen,
Die der kalte Nebel drückt,
Könnt' ich doch den Ausgang finden,
Ach, wie fühlt' ich mich beglückt!
Dort erblick' ich schöne Hügel,
Ewig jung und ewig grün!
Hätt' ich Schwingen, hätt' ich Flügel,
Nach den Hügeln zög ich hin.

Harmonieen hör' ich klingen,
Töne süßer Himmelsruh,
Und die leichten Winde bringen
Mir der Düfte Balsam zu,
Gold'ne Früchte seh ich glühen,
Winkend zwischen dunkelm Laub,
Und die Blumen, die dort blühen,
Werden keines Winters Raub.

Ach wie schön muß sich's ergehen
Dort im ew'gen Sonnenschein,
Und die Luft auf jenen Höhen
O wie labend muß sie seyn!
Doch mir wehrt des Stromes Toben,
Der ergrimmt dazwischen braußt,
Seine Wellen sind gehoben,
Daß die Seele mir ergraußt.

Einen Nachen seh ich schwanken,
Aber ach! der Fährmann fehlt.
Frisch hinein und ohne Wanken,
Seine Segel sind beseelt.
Du mußt glauben, du mußt wagen,
Denn die Götter leihn kein Pfand,
Nur ein Wunder kann dich tragen
In das schöne Wunderland.

Old Age Poem

by Sappho (630–580 B.C.),
from Ancient Greek by J. Simon Harris

Translator's Preliminary Note

This is an original translation of a poem by Sappho (630–580 B.C.), traditionally known as the "old age poem" or the "Tithonus poem." (In the standard numbering by Lobel and Page, it is "Fragment 58.") Tithonus, mentioned in the poem, was a mortal whom the goddess Dawn loved. She convinced Zeus to grant him eternal life, but neglected to ask for his eternal youth. A few words about the translation are warranted. The original poem has a complicated meter that is difficult to emulate in English. The hexameter of my poem is a poor man's substitute for Sappho's meter, but I hope it conveys a bit of the music nonetheless. In the same vein, my translation is not a word-for-word rendering, but more of an interpretation, intended to convey the music rather than the exact sense of the poem. The couplets of the original poem did not rhyme, as mine do; again, perhaps the rhyming will restore a bit of the music lost in translation. Finally, I want to note that the last four lines of my translation are drawn from fragments of the poem that appear only in one surviving manuscript; there is some scholarly debate as to whether those four lines should be part of the poem or not. In any case, my translation of them is very loose, since only fragments of those lines remain.

Hold on, little girls, to the beautiful gifts of the violet Muses,
and cling to your love of the clear sweet lyre, that lover of music.
My skin was once supple and smooth, but now it is withered by age;
my hair had been lustrous and black, but now it is faded and gray.
My heart grows heavy; my knees, too weary to stand upon,
though once, they could lift me and dance, and could leap as light as a fawn.
I grumble and groan on and on—and yet, what else can I do?
No woman has lived without aging, no man has eternal youth.
They say that Tithonus was held in the rosy arms of Dawn,
who carried him off to the ends of the earth, so her love would live on.
Though charming and young at the time, and despite his immortal wife,
he too would succumb to old age in the end of his endless life.
Yet, thinking of all that I've lost, I recall what maturity brings:
the wisdom I lacked as a youth, and a love for the finer things.
And Eros has given me beauty not found in the light of the sun:
the passion and patience for life that so often is lost on the young.

Old Age Poem
in Ancient Greek

ὔμμες πεδὰ Μοίσαν ἰ]ο̣κ[ό]λπων κάλα δῶρα, παῖδες,
σπουδάσδετε καὶ τὰ]ν φιλάοιδον λιγύραν χελύνναν·
ἔμοι δ᾽ ἄπαλον πρίν] ποτ᾽ [ἔ]οντα χρόα γῆρας ἤδη
ἐπέλλαβε, λεῦκαι δ᾽ ἐγ]ένοντο τρίχες ἐκ μελαίναν·
βάρυς δέ μ᾽ ὀ [θ]ῦμο̣ς πεπόηται, γόνα δ᾽ [ο]ὐ φέροισι,
τὰ δή ποτα λαίψηρ᾽ ἔον ὄρχησθ᾽ ἴσα νεβρίοισι.
τὰ (μὲν) στεναχίσδω θαμέως· ἀλλὰ τί κεν ποείην;
ἀγήραον ἄνθρωπον ἔοντ᾽ οὐ δύνατον γένεσθαι.
καὶ γάρ π[ο]τα̣ Τίθωνον ἔφαντο βροδόπαχυν Αὔων
ἔρωι φ̣. α̣θεισαν βάμεν᾽ εἰς ἔσχατα γᾶς φέροισα[ν,
ἔοντα̣ [κ]ά̣λ̣ον καὶ νέον, ἀλλ᾽ αὖτον ὔμως ἔμαρψε
χρόνωι πό̣λ̣ιο̣ν γῆρας, ἔχ[ο]ν̣τ̣᾽ ἀθανάταν ἄκοιτιν.
]ιμέναν νομίσδει
]αις ὀπάσδοι
ἔγω δὲ φίλημμ᾽ ἀβροσύναν, ...   ] τοῦτο καί μοι
τὸ λά[μπρον ἔρος τὠελίω καὶ τὸ κά]λον λέ[λ]ογχε.

The Ballad of Mulan

by an anonymous 6th-century poet,
from Chinese by Evan Mantyk

Sigh after sigh she sadly sighs
    While weaving near the door—
No sound of spinning loom that flies
    Just Mulan feeling poor.

Go ask her whom she thinks about,
    What boy is in her heart.
She says, "There's none I think about,
    There's no boy in my heart.

"Last night I saw the army's list
    Of those the Khan has picked.
On all twelve draft lists that exist
    My father's name is ticked.

"My father has no grown-up son
    Who can to battle race.
Once buying horse and saddle are done,
    I'll take my father's place."

She buys a fine steed in the East,
    A bridle in the South,
A saddle blanket in the West,
    A long whip in the North.

At dawn, to parents bids farewell,
    At dusk, to camp hello;
No sounds of their familiar yell,
    Just Yellow River flow.

At dawn, she leaves the Yellow River,
    At dusk, Black Mountains soar;
No sound of parents calling daughter,
    Just wild horsemen's roar.

Ten thousand miles for war she goes,
  Through mountain passes flying.
The sentry's gong on cold wind blows;
  Her iron armor's shining.

A hundred battles—generals die;
  In ten years, heroes surface
To meet the Emperor on high
  Enthroned in splendid palace.

He holds twelve scrolls that list their deeds,
  Gives thousands of rewards.
The Khan asks Mulan what she needs.
  "No titles fit for lords,"

She says, "To borrow a swift steed
  And ride home I prefer."
Her parents, hearing of this deed,
  Rush out to welcome her.

When older sister hears the news,
  She dresses, waits, and looks.
When younger brother hears the news,
  The swine and sheep he cooks.

She says, "The chamber door I open
  And sit upon my chair.
My wartime uniform is shaken;
  My old-time dress I wear."

She faces out the window, looking,
  Fixing cloudlike hair,
And turns then to the mirror, hooking
  Yellow flowers there.

Out of the gate she meets the men
　　Who'd by her side once fought.
For twelve years Mulan was a man,
　　Or so they all had thought!

The male hares' feet go hop and skip
　　And female hares look muddled,
But when they run at a good clip,
　　How can't one get befuddled?

木 蘭 詩

唧唧復唧唧，　木蘭當戶織。　不聞機杼聲，　唯聞女嘆息。
問女何所思？　問女何所憶？　”女亦無所思，女亦無所憶。
昨夜見軍帖，　可汗大點兵。　軍書十二卷，　卷卷有爺名。
阿爺無大兒，　木蘭無長兄。　願為市鞍馬，　從此替爺征。”
東市買駿馬，　西市買鞍韉，　南市買轡頭，　北市買長鞭。
朝辭爺娘去，　暮宿黃河邊。　不聞爺娘喚女聲，但聞黃河流水鳴濺濺。
旦辭黃河去，　暮至黑山頭。　不聞爺娘喚女聲，但聞燕山胡騎聲啾啾。
萬裡赴戎機，　關山度若飛。　朔氣傳金柝，　寒光照鐵衣。
將軍百戰死，　壯士十年歸。

歸來見天子，　天子坐明堂。　策勳十二轉，　賞賜百千強。
可汗問所欲，　”木蘭不用尚書郎，願借明駝千裡足，送兒還故鄉。”
爺娘聞女來，　出郭相扶將；阿姊聞妹來，　當戶理紅妝；
小弟聞姊來，　磨刀霍霍向豬羊。開我東閣門，坐我西閣床；
脫我戰時袍，　著我舊時裳；當窗理雲鬢，　對鏡帖花黃。
出門看火伴，　火伴皆驚惶。”同行十二年，不知木蘭是女郎。”
雄兔腳撲朔，　雌兔眼迷離。　雙兔傍地走，　安能辯我是雄雌？

210

A Snowy Day in Spring

by Yuan Xi, from Chinese by
Jennifer Zeng and Damian Robin

With all the trees in shrouds of falling snow,
We move toward the moment of Time's birth.
My thoughts leap forward with great strength and flow
Within the massive gap of heaven … earth.

Around me, cold East Wind that blows and blows
Much like a song—but who will sing with me?
Dispersing, wafting thoughts are vagrant echoes
Of Zi You gone, returned, now not with me.

I want to ride a donkey, sail the river
To trace plum blossoms at the edge of mind.
My thoughts reach gently, dancing on forever,
They leave the worried world's concerns behind.

While in the center of this pure white realm,
I could be in the presence of Ku Yi.
Contented, all my thoughts flow with no helm.
All I have is all I need to be.

*Zi You: A great Chinese calligrapher. Ku Yi: Refers to either a
Taoist mountain or a divine being who oversees the snow.*

春雪有懷

飛雪樹頭　太古周遊　我思浩浩　天地悠悠
東風吹徹　孰與唱酬　我思茫茫　不見子猷
尋梅策蹇　寒江泛舟　我思澹澹　聊以忘憂
四望一白　如臨姑射　我思渙渙　夫復何求

Autumn Wind

by Yuan Xi, from Chinese by
Jennifer Zeng and Damian Robin

From far off, Autumn wind runs at us in a rush!
Across a thousand miles, displacing clouds with sky,
(And crowding through the dark, tense soldiers in a hush)
Then past the cliff, through countless pines, like echoes fly.

秋風

遼天之末起秋風
千里長驅浮雲空
穿林初疑銜枚走
過崖猶響萬壑松

Snow in Spring

by Han Yu (768–824),
from Chinese by Jarek Zawadzki

Upon the New Year's Day no fragrant flowers came out,
Not till the second month did buds begin to sprout.
The snow humiliates the spring for being late,
And sprays white petals in the garden all about.

春雪

新年都未有芳华，
二月初惊见草芽。
白雪却嫌春色晚，
故穿庭树作飞花。

The Lake

by Alphonse de Lamartine (1790–1869),
from French by Michael Coy

Thus, ever driven onward to new shores, borne constantly away,
Can we never, in the Ocean of the Ages, drop anchor for a day?

Oh, this beautiful lake! The year has hardly flown,
yet here am I, beside these so-beloved waves of hers. Here, but alone.

Waves! You crashed against these rocks for her, white-blazing, beat
your heads against the wind, but also caressed her lovely feet.

One night—do you remember?—we lay here and felt
the rhythmic swish of oarsmen, slicing through your pelt.

That night was so enchanted, I swear to you I heard
accents never known on earth, as she let fall these words:

"Oh, Time, stop your flight! Hours, don't run away!
Allow us to savor this delight, the best of life's brief day!

So many unhappy ones implore you. Run, run for them.
Take, too, the cares which eat them up. But leave us, please, in pacem.

It's fruitless to complain, but these moments aren't enough:
I beg shy Night to linger, but look—bold Dawn scares her off.

So let us love, then. Let us love! Time cannot be caged.
Make haste: we'll strut our tiny hour, and then must quit the stage."

Jealous Time! Why do you rob with such frank eagerness
our days of joy, but dawdle when you see us in distress?

Why is it that we live and love, but leave no trace?
Why give us these raptures, which you then efface?

Eternity. Nothingness. The Past. Such somber chasms!
Where do you hide our human fire, our passion-prompted spasms?

214

Lake! Tall rocks! Oh, deep and secret woods! Nos amis!
Won't you keep of us at least some memory?

We live on in your calm, Sweet Lake, your storms, your laughing shores,
your gloomy pine trees, craggy rocks, through which the water roars.

It's in the summer wind we'll live, which ruffles as it kisses,
and in the single thoughtful star, which reflects and reminisces.

The rose which droops, the oak in ivy gloved,
the fragrance of the forest. These will tell the world, "They loved!"

Le Lac

Ainsi, toujours poussés vers denouveaux rivages,
Dans la nuit éternelle emportés sans retour,
Ne pourrons-nous jamais sur l'océan des âges
Jeter l'ancre un seul jour ?

Ô lac ! l'année à peine a fini sa carrière,
Et près des flots chéris qu'elle devait revoir,
Regarde ! je viens seul m'asseoir sur cette pierre
Où tu la vis s'asseoir !

Tu mugissais ainsi sous ces roches profondes,
Ainsi tu te brisais sur leurs flancs déchirés,
Ainsi le vent jetait l'écume de tes ondes
Sur ses pieds adorés.

Un soir, t'en souvient-il ? nous voguions en silence ;
On n'entendait au loin, sur l'onde et sous les cieux,
Que le bruit des rameurs qui frappaient en cadence
Tes flots harmonieux.

Tout à coup des accents inconnus à la terre
Du rivage charmé frappèrent les échos ;
Le flot fut attentif, et la voix qui m'est chère
Laissa tomber ces mots :

" Ô temps ! suspends ton vol, et vous, heures propices !
Suspendez votre cours :
Laissez-nous savourer les rapides délices
Des plus beaux de nos jours !

" Assez de malheureux ici-bas vous implorent,
Coulez, coulez pour eux ;
Prenez avec leurs jours les soins qui les dévorent ;
Oubliez les heureux.

" Mais je demande en vain quelques moments encore,
Le temps m'échappe et fuit ;
Je dis à cette nuit : Sois plus lente ; et l'aurore
Va dissiper la nuit.

" Aimons donc, aimons donc ! de l'heure fugitive,
Hâtons-nous, jouissons !
L'homme n'a point de port, le temps n'a point de rive ;
Il coule, et nous passons ! "

Temps jaloux, se peut-il que ces moments d'ivresse,
Où l'amour à longs flots nous verse le bonheur,
S'envolent loin de nous de la même vitesse
Que les jours de malheur ?

Eh quoi ! n'en pourrons-nous fixer au moins la trace ?
Quoi ! passés pour jamais ! quoi ! tout entiers perdus !
Ce temps qui les donna, ce temps qui les efface,
Ne nous les rendra plus !

Éternité, néant, passé, sombresabîmes,
Que faites-vous des jours que vous engloutissez ?
Parlez : nous rendrez-vous ces extases sublimes
Que vous nous ravissez ?

Ô lac ! rochers muets ! grottes ! forêt obscure !
Vous, que le temps épargne ou qu'il peut rajeunir,
Gardez de cette nuit, gardez, belle nature,
Au moins le souvenir !

Qu'il soit dans ton repos, qu'il soit dans tes orages,
Beau lac, et dans l'aspect de tes riants coteaux,
Et dans ces noirs sapins, et dans ces rocs sauvages
Qui pendent sur tes eaux.

Qu'il soit dans le zéphyr qui frémit et qui passe,
Dans les bruits de tes bords par tes bords répétés,
Dans l'astre au front d'argent qui blanchit ta surface
De ses molles clartés.

Que le vent qui gémit, le roseau qui soupire,
Que les parfums légers de ton air embaumé,
Que tout ce qu'on entend, l'on voit ou l'on respire,

Tout dise: Ils ont aimé !

Odysseus Strings His Bow

Excerpt from *The Odyssey*, by Homer, 21.388–22.125,
from Ancient Greek by Mike Solot

The cowherd, Philoetius, quickly but quietly slipped out
To fasten the gates of the courtyard. He picked up a rope
He had seen on the porch—a ship's cable made of papyrus—
And used it to lash down the bar, then went back inside
To the stool he had left. He sat with his eyes on Odysseus,
Now stroking the length of his bow, tapping it here,
Squeezing it there, turning it over and over
While feeling for holes in the horn—in case it was worm-eaten,
Riddled by grubs in the years he was lost in his wandering.

Some of the suitors were poking each other and saying,
"Look at the expert!" — "A beggar who really knows bows!" —
"I'll bet you he's hiding another one like it at home!" —
"Maybe he thinks he can make one!" — "A sponger, a tramp,
A master of misery, turning it this way and that!"
Another one, even more insolent, yelled to Odysseus:
"Bowmaking ought to be easy for someone like you—
As easy as stringing that big one you have in your hands!"

In spite of their jeering Odysseus gathered his wits
As he eyed his bow closely and hefted it, getting the feel—
Then quick, like a minstrel, a master of playing the lyre
Who easily stretches his sheep-gut up over the crossbar
And wraps it around in a fresh roll of oxhide to hold it,
So did Odysseus string the great bow, with effortless ease.
Shifting the grip to his right hand he tested the string
With a pluck: it twanged, shrill, like a twittering swallow.
The suitors fell silent, aghast, then their faces turned pale
As the deafening boom of a thunderbolt sounded above them—
Zeus, son of Crooked-Mind Cronus, was sending an omen
To splendid, enduring Odysseus. He listened, smiled,
And still sitting down, he picked up the one naked arrow
Eumaeus had left on his table; the others lay quiet,
Waiting, still in the quiver—but not for too long.

Odysseus and Telemachus pursuing suitors of Penelope
by Thomas Degeorge, 45.5 x 58.6 in., oil on canvas, 1812.

The suitors would sample them soon. Resting the shaft
At the grip of his bow he nocked it, drew back the string,
And aiming it closely, he fired: the bronze-heavy arrow flew
All the way through, clean, without even grazing
The tips of the handles. He instantly called out, "Telemachus!
Look! The stranger you welcomed to sit in your hall
As a guest didn't shame you. Did I have to struggle forever
To string it? Did I miss my aim—by even a little?
All those who mocked me were wrong. I still have my strength.
But now it is time we were giving these suitors their supper—
A supper in daylight. Why not? And then comes the fun:
The music, the dancing—whatever adorns a great feast."

He signaled his son with a look and a squinch of his brows.
Telemachus slung on his sword, then reached for his spear
In the rack by his throne—a javelin headed with bronze,
Its blade now aflame in the flickering light of the fire.

The master of guile, Odysseus, ripped off his rags.
Grabbing his bow and his quiver, chock-full of arrows,
He leapt to the threshold and emptied the shafts at his feet—
All were still pointed and fletched—then yelled to the suitors:
"Now that we've settled that contest, once and for all,
I'll try something new, a target no archer has touched.
Give me the glory, Apollo! Make my aim true!"

He sighted the sharp stabbing point of a shaft at Antinoûs
Just as the young man was lifting his elegant goblet,
A two-handled drinking-cup made out of gold, and embossed;
He nestled the bowl in his hands and was swirling the wine
Before taking a sip, unaware of the slaughter to come.
But why should he worry with so many feasters around him?
Who would imagine that one man alone against many,
No matter how brave, could dare to provoke such a fight—
Dooming himself to the dark, to a horrible death?
Odysseus picked out his spot at the base of the throat
And fired, hitting him square: the point and the shaft
Punched all the way through, leaving the feathers lodged deep
In the soft hollow pit of his thrapple. Antinoûs, stricken,
Pitched to the side as he let the cup fall from his hands,

Then suddenly kicked out a leg, upending his table
And spilling his dinner, his bread and his succulent meats,
Fouling it all with his blood—the lifeblood now spurting
In jets from his nostrils. As soon as they saw him tip over
The suitors all jumped from their chairs with an echoing roar,
Spinning around in a desperate search of the walls—
But there were no shields, no mighty spears to be grabbed.
Rage, and a fury of words—that's all they had
To hurl back at the stranger, with everyone screaming at once,
"You dare draw a bow on a lord?" — "Now you are done for!" —
"That shot was your last!" — "You cut down a prince, our best,
The noblest man on the island!" — "Vultures will eat you!"
So they supposed—the fools!—for each one was thinking
This man is no killer; he fired that shot by mistake!
They couldn't imagine that Death had them all by the throat.

Odysseus narrowed his eyes down to slits as he shouted back
"Dogs! You never believed it could happen—I'm home!
You thought I was lost after Troy so you looted my wealth,
You ravished my housemaids, dragging them into your beds,
And you brazenly wooed my own wife—while I was alive!—
As if you had nothing to fear from the gods or from men
And their vengeance—already afoot, but stalking behind you
Until it could strike. Now Death has you all by the throat!"

Cold sweaty Terror came over the suitors. It grabbed them,
Spinning them round once again—but now they were looking
For any way out. Only Eurymachus dared to speak back:
"If you are Odysseus, the Ithacan, finally home,
Then all that you say is quite fair. There have been offenses—
Outrages, yes!—many right here in this hall
And on your estates. But the culprit is already dead—
Antinoüs—he was the one! He is to blame!
He was the ringleader, egging on all of the others!
But he didn't lust for the marriage so much as the power—
That's what he wanted. He thought he could make himself king
Over all of the island by killing your son in an ambush—
But Zeus wouldn't let him, and gave him the death he deserved.
Spare us! We are your people! We'll go round our districts
And gather a levy of livestock and wine to repay you—
In full—for whatever we've eaten and drunk in your house.
And that isn't all. We'll make good the loss to your honor
By giving you treasures in bronze and in gold of our own—
Riches worth twenty good oxen from each man among us!
Now wouldn't that soften your temper? Of course, until then,
We all understand, you have every right to be angry."

Odysseus, glaring out balefully, answered, "Eurymachus!
Give me your riches, give me the wealth of your families,
All of them, all that they have, throw in your treasures
And taxes—not even then would I hold back my hands
From the work of revenge, not till you've paid for your wrongs
With your lives, every last one of you. Here is your choice:
Face me and fight, or escape—but I don't think you'll make it.
With Doom here already, Death can't be too far behind."

Each of them instantly felt his heart thunk in his chest
As he started to shake at the knees. Eurymachus shouted out
"Friends! He'll never let up with his murderous hands!
The bow and the threshold are his, and he'll fire those arrows
Until we're all dead! But think of the thrill of it—combat!
I say we all draw our swords, pick up our tables
To hold out as shields, and rush him together, at once,
Driving him down off the threshold, away from the doors,
So then we can run out and raise an alarm though the town.
The sooner we do it the sooner he shoots his last arrow!"

He drew his own sword, a finely honed, double-edged beauty,
Waggled the weapon, screeched out a war cry, then leapt
As he started to charge for the door—just at the moment
Odysseus fired an arrow that stuck in his chest,
Ripping down under his nipple and sinking its barbs
In the meat of his liver. Eurymachus let the sword drop,
Doubled, then crashed on his table, curling and writhing
And scattering food on the floor. The goblet went too.
His spasms of agony jerked him right over the edge
And he fell to the ground, taking it full on his forehead.
His legs were now twitching, both of them, kicking his chair
And making it rock as a mist filled his darkening eyes.

Now came Amphinomus, drawing his sword as he ran
At Odysseus, hoping to drive him away from the door—
But Telemachus got to him first with a spear in his back,
Hitting him square at the shoulders: it sunk in between them
And drove in so hard that the bronze came out bloody in front
As he fell forward flat, thumping the ground with his face.
Telemachus ran right around him, leaving his spear
Where it was, in Amphinomus, swaying and casting its shadows;
He was afraid if he bent down to wrench out the weapon
A suitor would jump him and hack him to death with his sword.
So he ran without stopping, sprinting as fast as he could,

And when he was up on the threshold he let his words fly:
"Father! I'll bring you a shield and two spears right away—
A helmet, all bronze, one that fits over your temples.
I'll shoulder my arms on the run and outfit the herdsmen
With all that they need. We've got to be ready to fight!"

Odysseus, his wits always working, answered him, "Run!
Go! Get back while I still have some arrows to shoot!
I can't hold this doorway without them—alone and unarmed!"
Obeying his father, Telemachus dashed to the storeroom,
The one where the armor was kept. He took out four shields,
Eight mighty spears, and four helmets—the helmets were bronze
And tasseled with horsehair—and ran back as fast as he could
To his father, still on the threshold, then put on his helmet
And shouldered his shield. Both of the herdsmen armed too.

All three took their stand by the cunning and deadly Odysseus
Who kept up his shower of arrows, aiming and firing
As long as they lasted, steadily picking off suitors;
One by one they went down, falling and dying
On top of each other, until all the arrows were gone.
Odysseus rested his bow in a nook by the doorjamb
And picked up his shield—a heavy one, four layers thick—
Slinging it over his shoulder. He pulled on his helmet
And tested the fit, shaking his powerful head,
Whipping the horsehair around with a terrible menace
While fisting a pair of his mighty, bronze-bladed spears.

VII. RIDDLES

Books and Birds by Laura Westlake, 10 x 12 in., oil on board, 2013.

A Brief History of Riddles

by Manfred Dietrich

The world is riddled with riddles. Riddling is as old and as ubiquitous as language itself. When God invited Adam to name the beasts and the beauties of creation, he showed that each naming was an answer to the universal riddle, "What am I called?"

Much later, somewhere east of Eden, many of the prophets worked in riddles: Daniel in Babylon could read the writing on the wall, and Solomon knew of that which "scattereth yet increaseth." Samson marked his wedding feast with a riddle for the Philistines: "Out of the eater came forth meat, and out of the strong came forth sweetness."

Among the Greeks, Oedipus had to solve the Riddle of the Sphinx. In *The Birds*, Aristophanes regards the lives of men as so many riddles. Aristotle sums it up: "The very nature indeed of a riddle is this, to describe a fact in an impossible combination of words (which cannot be done with the real names of things, but can be with their metaphorical substitutes)" (*Poetics*, 22). He elaborates further in his *Rhetoric* Book III: "Well-constructed riddles are attractive ... because the hearer expected something different, his acquisition of the new idea impresses him all the more" (Ch 11, 1412a).

After the Greeks and Romans, we find riddles used for both entertainment and knowledge among the Norse, the Celts, the Persians, and the Anglo-Saxons, many of whom regarded riddles as sources of wisdom. In this last group is Aldhelm, the earliest English writer whose works have survived, although it is only his Latin riddles and prose that remain, some of them preserved in the *Exeter Book*. His vernacular verse has vanished.

Aldhelm was born circa 639 to a West Saxon royal family. He flourished in the religious community at Canterbury, England. He founded a monastery at Bradford-on-Avon, and built there the Chapel of St. Lawrence, which still stands today. About 673, he became Abbot of Malmesbury. In 705, he became the first Bishop of Sherborne. He was an avid orator. He is reported to have sung songs and riddles on the bridge to attract an audience that might come to hear his sermons in the church. Much of this singing and riddling is said to have been secular rather than religious, giving him a wide appeal. Among his notable admirers were King Alfred and the Venerable Bede. Aldhelm was canonized. His feast day, May 25, is still marked at Malmesbury.

Riddles can be playful or profound, poetic and probing, or enchanting with trickery and misdirection. Every play of words that relishes sense and sound appeals to our innermost feelings. Consider the traveler who meets two men in a forest. One is bound to speak only truth, but his brother always lies. The traveler asks the first man, "Which one are you?" The first man replies, "My brother will tell you he is the truthful one." Layers of truth and deception unfold in an interesting way here. If the first brother is the liar, then the second brother must, in fact, say the opposite of what his brother predicts he would say. That, of course, is impossible since he must be the truthful brother if the first brother is the liar. Conversely, if the first brother is truthful, and the second brother is the liar, then, of course, the first brother will say truthfully that his liar brother will claim to be the truthful one.

Sure, it is stimulating to the mind (fun) to figure out these possibilities, but it also tells us something about the way words and the mind work. The second brother, who is the liar, draws attention to himself and becomes the center of focus, as lies and bad behavior often do in reality. Truth, however, ultimately reigns, as in all riddles.

Riddle I.

by Monty Phillips

I've never been exactly sure
How long I've been on this old earth;
It sometimes seems it's not much less
Than Man himself has held tenure.
I've took on many forms since birth
To keep abreast with Man's progress:

And took on many colors since
My nascent hue of bluey-black.
I started life in feathers, which
Necessitated many stints
In pots and wells (both with a lack
Of water). I then made the switch

To fountains (which also contained
No water). Since those days, my role
Has changed to stay by Man employed;
In recent times he's even trained
Me to work with jets. And a whole
New role began when redeployed

By Man (lest he makes a blunder)
To render me invisible!
I still retain my centuries-old
Propensity to get under
Man's skin… and it is risible
The cash he'll pay for this, I'm told.

I'd like to think I'm here to stay,
But Man's existence seems to be
Under threat. Well, if that's the case,
I wonder if there'll come a day
When Monkeys learn to work with me…
I could outlive the Human Race!

Riddle II.

Generations: An Interactive Riddle
(Who are "you" and "I"?)

by James B. Nicola

Your Great-Gran' was a prisoner and spent
Both day and night bound by a (double) chain.
Flies on the wall would swear he never went
Anywhere. But he didn't need a plane
To fly me to the farthest continent,
Nor liberty to lead me down the lane.

Your Gran' (a wizard too) would, in the car,
Lose all his magic powers, so I'd walk
Around with him indoors. His repertoire
Of words was not his own. That didn't shock
A single soul, though: Whose words ever are?
And flies on walls would swear he loved to talk.

Unchained but bound together, you and I
Now take each other anywhere we care
To go (and any way: We even fly
On aeroplanes as one). With ample air
There's ample magic, too, for those who buy.
Lately, though, it seems that everywhere
We go together (even in the sky),
Neither one of us is really there.

Envoi

If searching souls should find this riddle and
not print it out, nor read it on a screen
that's wider than a palm (as I have planned
for most), here's one more hint to what I mean:
As eyes peruse the problem now in hand,
"I's" also hold the answer, in between.
(If even still souls do not understand:
Solutions might be felt as well as seen.)

Riddle III.

by Remy Dambron

Due to my bipolar presence, I am both stormy and passive,
With solar winds and lunar lures, my surf-face rarely placid.
Fueling terrestrial climate, my wind and water are indispensable,
Even if at times, their devastation's indefensible.
I'm a beautiful beast of nature, who only remains the same by changing,
With my tempests, tides, and streams that I'm continually rearranging.
My forces aren't hormonal, they're by-products of a shared environment,
As a result the exchanges induced are passionate and violent.

Riddle IV.

by Amy Foreman

Capricious, shifting to-and-fro,
I'm sometimes fast and sometimes slow;
I've been around since long ago,
Yet I'm the one you cannot know.

A little of me lulls to sleep,
And when I stop, the sailors weep.
Too strong, and things lie in a heap:
The mess I make is never cheap.

I'll make you open windows wide,
Then slam them shut and stay inside.
On my account, will you decide
To button up, or bare your hide.

You'll never see me with your eye,
And yet you'll know when I pass by,
For rustling leaves will testify
When through the arbor, soft, I fly.

Little Yellow Bird by Laura Westlake, 8 x 8.5 in, oil on board, 2018.

Riddle V.

by Fr. Bruce Wren

You can hear me in the canyons,
    But not upon the sea,
The most likely of companions
    If you but cry to me.

Riddle VI.

by Connor Rosemond

What pounds and plods as if with toes,
And utilizes stress?
What's out of favor, out of style,
Yet we use, neverthless?

Riddle VII.

by Rohini Sunderam

What are you?
Blue or brown or green or gray
Are you a flower?
Yea and nay!
You do not teach
You do not preach
Yet, if I'm right
You control the light
Found on every creature's face
Especially the human race
But, as a flower this is true
Most often, you'll be wearing blue

Riddle VIII.

by Jennifer Hinders

We eat it hot, we eat it cold,
And sometimes we eat it with mold.

It's hard, it's soft, and in between,
If we're asked to do this—it isn't mean.

The Brits say it for a bit of wind,
Others talk about it when we grin.

Bars, balls, or giant wheels,
Or someone who doesn't act real

Now that's a lot of clues, you see
So what is the answer to this riddle, please?

Riddle IX.

by Zachary Dilks

That's just like me to set down roots
Wherever I go
Is wherever I grow
They'll whisper me wishes and give the boot
To carry their secrets wherever I blow

Riddle X.

by Ram

Your right is my left, your left is my right,
No one can see me when there is no light.

When you cry, I cry, when you smile, I smile,
Whatever you do, I do it in style!

Your moves and actions, I capture with ease,
Your words I can't match, I can't speak back please!

I am not your lost twin, I am not your soulmate,
How then your actions, I do emulate?

You check with me to make sure you are fine,
Who am I? Tell me, while there is sunshine!

Riddle XI.

by Manfred Dietrich

From small beginnings I grow great,
just keep up the heat and wait,
help me become the thing I am,
give me all the heat you can.

Let me transform the gathered dew
and I'll transform the world for you.
Tend me well from hour to hour
and I'll reward you with vast power.

Vast clouds of strength, yours to command,
as I grow greater and expand,
can carry you to distant lands
across oceans and desert sands,
propel you to heights or turn on your lights,
but don't neglect me—I can explode.
Heed my whistle when it blows.

Riddle XII.

by Nicky Hetherington

My first is in tick and also in tock.
My second's in minutes, but not in clock.
My third is in moments and millennia.
My fourth is in eons and also era.

I watch worlds being born, grow old, wither and die,
I can seem to stand still, or, without wings, to fly.
I was at the beginning; I'll be at the end,
I may be your companion, but never your friend.

What am I?

Riddle XIII.

by Manfred Dietrich

We carry clouds until we die
Though cut for crutches, death means little
Since support is the trade we ply
And on our shoulders sparrows nestle.
We nurture children carefully
Upon our very fingertips,
But the first night that's summery,
We scatter them from moonlit grips.

We challenge geometric space
And have no need of gravity,
For earth and air and wind we grace.

Riddle XIV.

by Manfred Dietrich

I'm born in prison and cannot leave,
And yet unbound by space or time.
Though the door's unbolted I can't heave
It open till the jailer dies.
I travel with him forced to follow,
Though he's lost without me here.
Should I die one day he'd also.
To me, his slave, he must adhere.

Riddle Answers:

I. Ink;
II. Cell or mobile phone, person holding it;
III. Oceans;
IV. Wind;
V. Echo;
VI. Meter;
VII. Iris;
VIII. Cheese;
IX. Dandelions;
X. Mirror image;
XI. Steam;
XII. Time;
XIII. Tree;
XIV. Soul

2019 POETRY COMPETITION WINNERS

First Place ($1,000 Prize): Adam Sedia, Indiana
"Arise, You Bones" "To Xi" "Let None Dare Call It Beauty"

Second Place: Joseph Charles MacKenzie, New Mexico
"To Nicholas Wilton" "Letter to England (For Tommy Robinson)" "Ode to the Great Highland Pipes"

Second Place: Amy Foreman, Arizona
"Let's Take the Other Bus" "Time for the B.S.: Susie and Johnny Go to College"

Third Place: James A. Tweedie, Washington State
"The Cost of Higher Education" "Of Roland and of Kings"
"The Seven Wonders of the Ancient World And What Became of One of Them"

Third Place: Sally Cook, New York
"Star Needles" "One Day In May" "How My Scientific Bent Got Broken"

Third Place: Joe Tessitore, New York
"Subversive Rhyme" "The Ballerina" "The Dance of Life"

Fourth Place: Daniel Leach, Texas
"The Snowflake" "It..." "Ode to Spring Mourning"

Fourth Place: Charlie Bauer, North Carolina
"Weaknesses" "Statues" "A Question of Faith"

Fourth Place: Annabelle Fuller, England
"The Architect"

Honorable Mention

Jeffrey Essmann, New York: "The Birth of Beauty" "Like Wordsworth's Humble Nun" "This Sonnet Has Been Funded by the State"

Peter Hartley, England: "The Fate of Fine Art" "The Dark Ages" "Poetry Today"

Dusty Grein, Northwest USA: "An Open Letter to the Librarian of Congress Carla Hayden"

Martin Rizley, Spain: "The Pale Rider Comes" "American Apocalypse"

Translation

First Place ($100 Prize): Martin Hill Ortiz, Puerto Rico
"Farewell to the Royal Gardens at Aranjuez" by María Rosa Gálvez de Cabrera

Second Place: David Gosselin, Quebec, Canada
"The Feast of Belshazzar" by Heinrich Heine

Second Place: Michael Coy, Spain
"The Lake" by Alphonse de Lamartine

Third Place: Charles Eager, England
"Du Bist Mein" by Anonymous; "The Golden Sun" by Georg Weerth; "An Elegy for His Brother" by Cattallus (Carmen VI)

Third Place: Jarek Zawadzki
"Snow in Spring" by Han Yu

Third Place: Luigi Pagano
"Alla Sera" by Ugo Foscolo

High School

First Place ($100 Prize): Victor Tyne, St. Peter's Preparatory School; Jersey City, New Jersey
"In Memory of Romeo and Juliet"

Second Place: Rhea Mitr, Quarry Lane School; Dublin, California
"My Somber Saunter"

Second Place: Deborah Ogunsanwo, St. Bedes High School;
"Made in China"

Third Place: Kaley Henyon, Linganore High School;
Frederick, Maryland
"The Forest"

Third Place: Jacyln Kennedy, Cactus Shadows High School;
Cave Creek, Arizona
"Creed of Communism"

Judges

Joseph S. Salemi,
Evan Mantyk

All winning poems appear in this Journal and/or on the Society's website

ARTISTS
Contemporary Painters & Sculptors

Armusik, Eric is a painter of classical figurative art continuing the tradition of epic storytelling. He is present online at EricArmusik.com

Bain, Anna Rose is a classically trained painter and portrait artist based in Denver, Colorado. She can be found online at ArtworkByAnnaRose.com

Dong, Xiqiang is a classically trained painter of Chinese origins and a Falun Gong practitioner.

Gussin, Clark Louis is a naturalistic painter in the classic tradition of portrait, landscape, still life, and genre, and can be found online at ClarkGussinArt.com

Howard, Sabin is a classically trained sculptor who specializes in mythologically and historically themed artworks. His website is sabinhoward.com

Hunter, Abraham is a painter specialized in creating photorealistic landscapes, oftentimes with spiritual connotations drawing on Christian perspectives. His works can be viewed at InfinityFineArt.com/Abraham Hunterartgallery.php

Keathley, Mark is a realistic painter specialized in landscapes as well as Western and wildlife art. More information about his work is presented at MarkKeathley.com

Levin, Steven J. is a classical realist painter living in Minneapolis, Minnesota, whose webpage is StevenJLevin.com

Pfeiffer, Jacob A. is a realistic painter whose work focuses on still lifes. He lives in Madison, Wisconsin, and displays images of his paintings at JacobAPfeiffer.com

Schlenker, Robert is a painter specialized in landscape and wildlife art, whose naturalistic works can be observed at BigSkyWildlifeArt.com

Seward, Steven is a painter following the classical artistic tradition and focusing on realistic portraits. He is based in Cleveland and is present online at StevenSewardPortraits.com

Shen, Daci is a classically trained painter of Chinese origins and a Falun Gong practitioner.

Smorenburg, Herman is a Dutch painter focusing on the creation of realistic paintings with symbolic connotations. His website is HermanSmorenburg.com

Westlake, Laura is a painter specialized in creating landscapes and still lifes, whose classically crafted artworks are inspired by the natural world. She lives in Orient, New York, and is also present online at LauraWestlake.net

Painters from the Past

Becker, Ferdinand (*1846–1877*) was a German painter mainly representing narratives through his work.

Blake, William (*1757–1827*) was not only a Romantic English poet but also a classically oriented painter and printmaker.

Butler, Charles Ernest (*1864–circa 1933*) was a British painter who specialized in portraits, landscapes, and mythologically themed artworks.

Cole, Thomas (*1801–1848*) was an English-born American painter well known for creating landscapes, wildlife, and historically themed paintings. He is considered to be the founder of the Hudson River School.

David, Jacques-Louis (*1748–1825*) was a French neoclassical painter, appreciated for his paintings depicting historical scenes.

Degeorge, Thomas (*1786–1854*) was a French neoclassical painter, known for his depictions of historical and religious scenes, as well as for portraits and rural landscapes.

Lucas, Auger (*1685–1765*) was a classically trained French painter, who mostly focused on creating artworks with mythological themes.

Taunay, Nicolas-Antoine (*1755–1830*) was a French painter known for his representations of mythological, religious, and historical scenes.

van Utrecht, Adriaen (*1599–1652*) was a Flemish painter generally known for his rich banquet, fruit, and game still lifes, as well as for his depictions of market, kitchen, and farmyard scenes.

POETS

Anderson, C.B. was the longtime gardener for the PBS television series *The Victory Garden*. Hundreds of his poems have appeared in scores of print and electronic journals out of North America, Great Britain, Ireland, Austria, Australia, and India. His collection *Mortal Soup and the Blue Yonder* was published in 2013 by White Violet Press.

Bardwell, Caroline is a resident and native of upstate New York. She is a professional geologist, a mother, a woman of faith, and a lover of music, art, literature, and nature. She has a great appreciation for the structural guidelines and musicality of formal verse.

Bauer, Charles resides in Apex, North Carolina, and is a salesman for a commercial carpet manufacturer.

Blanchard, Jane lives and writes in Georgia. One of her sonnets recently won the inaugural Letheon Poetry Prize. She has two collections—*Unloosed* and *Tides & Currents*—both with Kelsay Books.

Burd, Jr., Randal A. is an educator, freelance editor, writer, and poet. His freelance writing includes assignments on the paid writing team for Ancestry.com and multiple online blogs, newsletters, and publications. Randal received his master's degree in English Curriculum and Instruction from the University of Missouri. He currently works on the site of a residential treatment facility for juveniles in rural Missouri. He lives in southeast Missouri with his wife and two children.

Canerdy, Janice is a retired high-school English teacher from Potts Camp, Mississippi. Her first book, *Expressions of Faith* (Christian Faith Publishing), was published in December 2016.

Cherub, Kim is a devout Catholic, an unapologetic conservative, and a lover and patron of the fine arts. She has been writing poetry for more than twenty years, but has only recently begun to submit her work for publication.

Clark, Florence Adams spent her early childhood in the Rocky Mountain mining town of Gilman, Colorado. She left Colorado to attend Wellesley College, graduating in 1949 and moving with her husband to Ithaca, New York, where she raised a family and taught high school English. She has been writing poetry for as long as she can remember.

Clickard, C.L. is an internationally published poet and award-winning children's author. You can find more about her work at both CLClickard.com and her evil twin ClariceRadrick.com

Coates, Margaret lives in California. Long ago, she earned a Ph.D. in English and American literature and language, but left the academic field for a better position schooling her own children. She has continued to help other homeschooling families with courses in literature and Latin, and she sings in choirs for the Traditional Latin Mass.

Cook, Sally is a former Wilbur Fellow and six-time Pushcart nominee. She is a regular contributor to *National Review*, and has appeared in various venues, including *Trinacria*. Also a painter, her present works in the style known as Magic Realism are represented in national collections such as the NSDAR Museum in Washington, D.C., and the Burchfield Penney Art Center in Buffalo, New York.

Coy, Michael, a barrister, teacher, and journalist, is an Irish poet who has settled permanently in the south of Spain. He readily admits to a serious rhyme-and-rhythm habit. He is winner of various poetry prizes in Britain and Ireland.

Curtis, Michael has 40 years of experience in architecture, sculpture, and painting. He has taught and lectured at universities, colleges, and museums, including The Institute of Classical Architecture and The National Gallery of Art, et cetera. His pictures and statues are housed in over 400 private and public collections, including The Library of Congress, The Supreme Court, et alibi; his verse has been published in over 20 journals, his most recent book in prose, *Classical Architecture and Monuments of Washington, D.C.: A History and Guide*, 2018, The History Press. Mr. Curtis consults on scholarly, cultural, and artistic projects, currently: curator, Plinth & Portal; co-director, The Anacostia Project; vice-president, Liberty Fund, D.C.; lead designer on the 58-square-mile city of AEGEA.

Dambron, Remy is a former English teacher in California, who has taken time off to write.

Darling, Jan is a New Zealander who has worked in Auckland, Wellington, London, Barcelona, New York, and Sydney at copywriting and marketing strategy. She has spent her leisure time over 60 years writing poetry and short stories. Now retired, she lives in pastoral New South Wales with her husband, Arturo.

Dietrich, Manfred is a senior, semi-retired from a business career, living in Hamilton, Canada. He received degrees in English Literature in the 1970s, whereupon he went to England as a Commonwealth Scholar and a Canada Council for the Arts scholar to pursue doctoral research on the poetry of Matthew Arnold.

Dilks, Zachary is a writer currently residing just outside of Austin, Texas. A toolmaker by trade and a poet by heart, he began pursuing his passion for writing at age 17.

Essmann, Jeffrey is a writer whose prose work has appeared in *The New York Times*, *The Washington Post*, and numerous magazines and literary journals. He lives in New York City.

Foreman, Amy hails from the southern Arizona desert, where she homesteads with her husband and seven children. She has enjoyed teaching both English and music at the college level, but is now focused on home-schooling her children, gardening, farming, and writing. Recently, she has launched a blog of her poetry, The Occasional Caesura: A Pause Midline (TheOccasionalCaesura.WordPress.com).

Gilliland, Sam resides in Scotland where he is a champion of Lallans (Scottish language) poetry and a recipient of Sangschaw's prestigious MacDiarmid Tassie. With three previous collections of poetry published, his work in Scots includes *A Rickle O Banes* (Penny Wheep Press). He is founder and secretary of the Ayrshire Writers & Artists Society, the organization that became the home of The Scottish International Open Poetry Competition, to which he devoted 28 years of his life as co-administrator and judge.

Goldberg, Lee (aka Rantingsenior) is a writer who lives in Naperville, Illinois. He is retired, 72 years old, and has worked in a variety of areas including computer programming and network administration.

Gosselin, David Bellemare is a student in classics and languages in Montreal. His poetry, translations, and essays can be read on TheChainedMuse.com

Grein, Dusty is an author, poet, and graphics designer from Federal Way, Washington. His most recent book of poetry is *A Mist Shrouded Path* (RhetAskew Publishing, 2018). His blog, From Grandpa's Heart (GrandpasHeart.Blogspot.com), is followed by fans around the world.

Harris, J. Simon lives with his family in Raleigh, North Carolina. He is a graduate researcher in Materials Science at NC State University. Much of his poetry, including his ongoing translation of Homer's *Iliad* in dactylic hexameter and samples of his translation of Dante's *Inferno* in terza rima, is available on his website (JSimonHarris.com). His novel, *Lemnos*, is available now on Amazon Kindle.

Hartley, Peter is a retired painting restorer. He was born in Liverpool and lives in Manchester, UK.

Hay, C. David is a retired dentist living in Indiana and Florida. He received his B.S. and Doctor of Dental Surgery degrees from Indiana University. He is the author of five books of poetry which are dedicated to his wife, Joy. He has been widely published nationally and abroad and his poetry has been read on the British Broadcasting Channel. He has been nominated for the Pushcart Prize in Poetry and is the recipient of the Ordo Honoris Award from Kappa Delta Rho.

Hayes, Ted was a university faculty (Ph.D. in political science from the University of California 1967) and freelancer in his early career. He moved into full-time journalism and is now retired.

Hetherington, Nicky lives in Mid-Wales, UK, where she writes and performs her poems, as well as working in the education sector. Nicky won the Poetry Prize in the Oriel Davies Open Writing Competition 2017 and 2nd Prize in *Writing Magazine*'s Haiku competition. She has published a collection titled *Cultivating Caterpillars*, which is available to order from her website at Nicky-Hetherington.weebly.com

Hinders, Jennifer lives outside Washington, D.C. She's an instructional assistant and part-time freelance writer. To see her publications, view her website at JHinders.com

Hodges, Ron L. is an English teacher and poet who lives in Orange County, California. He won the Society's prestigious Annual Poetry Competition in 2016.

Holbrook, Rachel writes from her home in Knoxville, Tennessee. She is the author of the syndicated serial *Little River*. She was recently awarded an Honorable Mention by the International English Honor Society Sigma Tau Delta at their annual English convention for her short story "A Slow Burn," and received the Springs of Helicon Poetry Award from the English faculty at Tennessee Wesleyan University. She can be found online at RachelHolbrook.net

Hyatt, Jenni Wyn, née Williams, was born in Maesteg, South Wales, UK, in 1942. She worked as an English teacher in Worcestershire for many years before moving to Ceredigion in Wales, where she worked as a freelance family history researcher. She now lives in Derbyshire with her husband, Pete, and cat, Mabon. Her first collection, *Perhaps One Day*, was published in 2017.

Jackson, K.G. is retired from the mental health field, resides in Elmhurst, Illinois, and enjoys the written word in all its forms.

Juster, A.M. is the penname of Michael J. Astrue, an American lawyer, poet, editor, and critic. He served as Commissioner of the U.S. Social Security Administration from 2007 to 2013. Since fall 2018, he has served as Poetry Editor of *First Things*. His books include *Longing for Laura* (Birch Brook Press, 2001); *The Secret Language of Women* (University of Evansville Press, 2003); *The Satires of Horace* (University of Pennsylvania Press, 2008); *Tibullus' Elegies* (Oxford University Press, 2012); and *Saint Aldhelm's Riddles* (University of Toronto Press 2015). He has won the Howard Nemerov Sonnet Award three times, the Richard Wilbur Award, the Willis Barnstone Translation Prize and received other recognition, including two honorary degrees.

Karthik, Nivedita is a graduate in Integrated Immunology from the University of Oxford who likes reading books and traveling. She is an accomplished Bharatanatyam dancer and has given many performances. She loves any form of creative writing (especially poems) and writes them whenever she can.

King, Martin John is a retiree living in Somerset, England.

Krusch, William is a first-year English major at the University of North Carolina at Chapel Hill; he hails from Greensboro, North Carolina.

Krushyna, Ryhor is a Belarusian poet whose poetry has been translated by his son, Ihar Kazak (pseudonym of Igor Gregory Kozak), a poet-writer and literary translator, who has translated from Russian such émigré authors as Artsibashev, Averchenko, Teffi, et al, and from Belarusian: Bykov, Levanovich, Skobla, et al. In the poetry field, Ihar Kazak was awarded the Gabo Prize for Translation of Poetry for 2018.

La Rosa, Ralph C. was a Senior Lecturer in the USSR, at Tbilisi State University, SSR of Georgia. His work has been published online and in print, including the chapbook *Sonnet Stanzas* and full-length *Ghost Trees*.

Lauretta, M.P. lives in the UK. She is a humanities graduate and first became acquainted with prosody while in higher education in London. However, it wasn't until several years later that she decided to take up the challenge of writing formal poetry with rhyme and meter, quickly developing a special predilection for the exacting but elegant form of the Shakespearean sonnet. Her first collection, titled *To a Blank Page and Other Poems*, contains 28 original poems, 15 of which are Shakespearean sonnets. Her book is available from Amazon, Apple iBooks, and Barnes & Noble.

Leach, Daniel is a poet living in Houston, Texas. He has spent much of his life fighting for the ideals of classical culture and poetry.

Libby, Father Richard is a priest of the Diocese of Corpus Christi, in Texas.

Lukey, Benjamin Daniel was born in 1986. He has lived all over the Eastern United States and currently resides near Charlotte, North Carolina. He teaches high school English classes whenever he is not fishing or writing poetry.

MacKenzie, Joseph Charles is a traditional lyric poet, First Place winner of the Scottish International Poetry Competition (Long Poem Section). His poetry has appeared in various major news outlets, including *The New York Times*, *The Scotsman* (Edinburgh), *The Independent* (London), *US News and World Report*, and Google News.

Magdalen, Daniel is a doctoral student in the Faculty of Letters at the University of Bucharest, in Romania.

Maibach, Michael Charles began writing poems at age nine. Since then he has continued writing poems, and sharing them with friends. In November 2015 he opened a Facebook page—Poems of Michael Charles Maibach. It offers 140 poems written since then. His career has involved global business diplomacy. He is a native of Peoria, Illinois. Today Michael resides in Old Town Alexandria, Virginia.

Mantyk, Evan teaches history and literature in the Hudson Valley region of New York, where he lives with his wife and two children. He is president of The Society of Classical Poets.

Martin, Lynn Michael is a student of British literature who lives in Hagerstown, Maryland. He has a special interest in the sonnet and the Romantic poets. He is a student editor of *Hedge Apple* magazine.

McQuade, Tonya is an English teacher at Los Gatos High School in Los Gatos, California, and lives with her husband in San Jose, California. She has been writing poetry since fourth grade and is currently a member of Poetry Center San Jose.

Mertz, Carole, a professional musician, turned to writing 10 years ago. Her poems won several Wilda Morris Poetry Challenges in 2015. Carole resides with her husband in Parma, Ohio.

Miller, Avery was once a high school Spanish teacher and is now a home educator in New York. She and her husband are much occupied with math, meals, science, soccer games, sentence diagrams, dirty dishes, Latin, and laundry.

Myers, Tim J. is a writer, songwriter, storyteller, and senior lecturer at Santa Clara University. His children's books have won recognition from *The New York Times*, NPR, and the Smithsonian; he has 16 out and more on the way. He's published over 140 poems, won a first prize in a poetry contest judged by John Updike, has three books of adult poetry out with one in press, published a nonfiction book on fatherhood, and won a major prize in science fiction. He won the West Coast Songwriters Saratoga Chapter Song of the Year and the 2012 SCBWI Magazine Merit Award for Fiction. Find him at TimMyersStorySong.com or on Facebook at facebook.com/TimJMyers1

Narayana, Sathya, once a lawyer, joined the government of India as Inspector of Salt in 1984 and got two service promotions. In May 2014, he took voluntary retirement as Superintendent of Salt.

Nicola, James B. is a writer whose nonfiction book *Playing the Audience* won a Choice award. His two poetry collections, published by Word Poetry, are *Manhattan Plaza* (2014) and *Stage to Page: Poems from the Theater* (2016). He won a Dana Literary Award, a People's Choice award (from *Storyteller* magazine), and a *Willow Review* award; was nominated twice for a Pushcart Prize and once for a Rhysling Award; and was featured poet in *The New Formalist*. A Yale graduate as well as a composer, lyricist, and playwright, James has been giving both theater and poetry workshops at libraries, literary festivals, schools, and community centers all over the country. His children's musical *Chimes: A Christmas Vaudeville* premiered in Fairbanks, Alaska, where Santa Claus was rumored to be in attendance on opening night.

O'Shea, Sheri-Ann is a South African-born teacher now living in Brisbane, Australia, with her husband and three lively boys.

Peterson, Roy E. is an author, former diplomat, and retired U.S. Army Military Intelligence and Russian Foreign Area Officer who currently resides in Texas.

Philipp, Joshua is a journalist living in New York City. He is Vice President and Chief Technology Officer of The Society of Classical Poets.

Phillips, Connie is a former English teacher and editor living in Massachusetts.

Phillips, Monty is a 54-year-old driver who grew up in England, but he's been living in Provence (France) for the last 17–18 years. He also spends three months every year in Nepal.

Ram is a poet living in Mumbai, India.

Ramirez, Andrew Todd is a writer and full-time student at Texas A&M University in College Station, Texas. He is 27 years old and first began writing poetry after reading "For Whom the Bell Tolls" by John Donne.

Ream, Alexander King is a poet living in Tennessee. A member of the Demosthenian Literary Society at the University of Georgia, he deployed to Hawaii, then wrote on Lookout Mountain, continuing with Delta Kappa Epsilon International. Berkeley, Ann Arbor, and Athens encouraged him as a writer.

Robin, Damian lives in England, where he works as a copyeditor and proofreader. He lives with his wife and two of their three adult children. He won Second Place in the Society's 2014 Poetry Competition.

Rodriguez, Ramón, LC, is a religious brother studying for the priesthood. He is currently completing his degree in Classical Humanities in Cheshire, Connecticut.

Rosemond, Connor is an 18-year-old poet from North Carolina.

Ruleman, William is professor of English at Tennessee Wesleyan College. His books include two collections of his own poems (*A Palpable Presence* and *Sacred and Profane Loves*, both from Feather Books), as well as the following volumes of translation: *Poems from Rilke's Neue Gedichte* (WillHall Books, 2003), *Vienna Spring: Early Novellas and Stories of Stefan Zweig* (Ariadne Press, 2010), and, from Cedar Springs Books, *Verse for the Journey: Poems on the Wandering Life by the German Romantics*, *A Girl and the Weather* (poems and prose of Stefan Zweig), and *Selected Poems of Maria Luise Weissmann*.

Ruskovich, Mike lives in Grangeville, Idaho. He taught high school English for 36 years. He and his wife have four children.

Sale, James, FRSA, is a leading expert on motivation, and the creator and licensor of Motivational Maps worldwide. James has been writing poetry for over 40 years and has seven collections of poems published, including most recently, *Inside the Whale*, his metaphor for being in a hospital and surviving cancer, which afflicted him in 2011. He can be found at the website JamesSale.Co.uk and contacted at james@motivationalmaps.com. He is the winner of First Prize in the Society's 2017 Competition and Second Prize in the Society's 2015 Competition.

Salemi, Joseph S. has published five books of poetry, and his poems, translations, and scholarly articles have appeared in over 100 publications worldwide. He is the editor of the literary magazine *Trinacria*. He teaches in the Department of Humanities at New York University and in the Department of Classical Languages at Hunter College.

Sandler, Sally is a writer and graduate of the University of Michigan. She lives in San Diego, California.

Sedia, Adam (b. 1984) lives in his native Northwest Indiana, where he practices law as a civil and appellate litigator. He has had short stories and works of legal scholarship published in various journals. He also composes music, which may be heard on his YouTube channel.

Shaffer, Steven usually engages in the art form of computer code, which supports his poetry habit. He lives in a suburb of the middle of nowhere in central Pennsylvania with his wife and two dogs. His blog is My So-Called Civilization (MySoCalledCivilization.wordpress.com)

Shook, Don, former president of the Fort Worth Poetry Society and founder of The Actors Company, is a writer, actor, director, and producer. He has performed in theater, film, and television across the country, including opera at Carnegie Hall in New York, and as resident performer at Casa Mañana Musicals in Fort Worth and Six Flags Over Texas in Arlington. He is an award-winning author who recently published novels *Bluehole* and *Detour* and four poetry books, and was selected 2009 Senior Poet Laureate of Texas. Don Shook Productions offers shows ranging from murder mysteries to musical reviews: ShookShows.com

Solot, Mike was born in Tucson, Arizona, where he now lives. His translation of Homer's *Odyssey* is nearly completed.

Spring, Joe lives and works in Johannesburg, South Africa. For more information please visit JoeSpringWrites.com

Sugar, Alan shares his poetry and performance art in Decatur, Georgia, where he currently resides. He is also a puppeteer, and he has worked as a special education teacher in the public schools of Atlanta. Currently, Alan works as a writing tutor at Georgia State University Perimeter College, Clarkston Campus.

Sunderam, Rohini is a Canadian of Indian origin. She is a semi-retired advertising copywriter whose articles and stories have appeared in *The Statesman* (Calcutta, India) *The Globe & Mail* (Canada), and *The Halifax Chronicle Herald* (Nova Scotia, Canada) in addition to several Bahrain-based publications. As Zohra Saeed, she is the author of *Desert Flower* (Ex-L-Ence Publishing, UK). She was a contributor to the anthologies *My Beautiful Bahrain* (Miracle Publishing, Bahrain), *More of My Beautiful Bahrain*, and *Poetic Bahrain* (Robin Barratt Publishing, UK), and *Corpoetry*—a collection of poems satirizing corporate life (Ex-L-Ence Publishing).

Tessitore, Joe is a retired New York City resident and poet.

Tweedie, James A. is a recently retired pastor living in Long Beach, Washington. He likes to walk on the beach with his wife. He has written and self-published four novels and a collection of short stories. He has several hundred unpublished poems tucked away in drawers.

Tyne, Victor is a high school junior at St. Peter's Preparatory School in Jersey City, New Jersey, where he writes for the school newspaper, *The Petroc*. With an interest in classical languages, he hopes to pursue his passion for classics in the future. He currently resides with his family in Caldwell, New Jersey.

Van Inman, Clinton was born in Walton-on-Thames, England, in 1945. He graduated from San Diego State University in 1977 and is now a retired high school English teacher in Tampa Bay, Florida, where he lives with his wife, Elba.

Wang, Anthony is a high school student in Toronto.

Watt, David is a writer from Canberra, the "Bush Capital" of Australia. When not working for IP (Intellectual Property) Australia, he finds time to appreciate the intrinsic beauty of traditional rhyming poetry. He was the First Place winner in the Friends of Falun Gong Poetry Contest 2018.

Whidden, Phillip is a poet published in America, England, Scotland (and elsewhere) in book form, online, and in journals.

Whippman, David is a British poet, now retired after a career in healthcare. Over the years he's had quite a few poems, articles, and short stories published in various magazines.

Wilson, André Le Mont morphed into a poet, writer, songwriter, and storyteller soon after his parents, both poets, died in 2012 eleven weeks apart, bequeathing him hundreds of poems. He performs around the San Francisco Bay Area where he lives.

Wise, Bruce Dale (aka BDW) is a poet living in Texas who often writes under anagrammatic heteronyms. He won First Prize in the Society of Classical Poets' 2014 Competition.

Wren, Fr. Bruce, born in 1962 in the small town of Cottonwood, Idaho, currently serves as chaplain of the Chicago Chapter of the Lumen Institute, section director of the Chicago Regnum Christi Men's section, chaplain to the Catholic Professionals of Illinois, spiritual director for many religious and lay people, and helps regularly at several parishes in the Chicago Diocese. He also devotes regular time to the female congregations of the Missionaries of Charity, the Little Sisters of the Poor, and the Rosary Hill Dominican Sisters. He has published one book of poetry, *Fending off the Dragon Fire,* available at Amazon.

Xi, Yuan is a poet, columnist, and screenwriter. She was forced to leave China after being persecuted by the Chinese Communist Party for her belief in Falun Dafa. She currently lives in the United States and writes columns, poetry, commentaries, and articles about Chinese history for a number of overseas publications. She also writes TV drama series scripts for New Realms Studios in Canada.

Yankevich, Leo was a poet who was born in Pennsylvania and lived in Poland. His latest books are *The Last Silesian* (The Mandrake Press, 2005), *Tikkun Olam & Other Poems* (Second Expanded Edition; Counter-Currents Publishing, 2012), and *Journey Late at Night: Poems & Translations* (Counter-Currents Publishing, 2013). He was editor of *The New Formalist*. More of his work can be found at LeoYankevich.com. He passed away in December 2018.

Zanelli, Alessio is an Italian poet who writes in English and whose work has appeared in over 150 literary journals from 13 countries. He has published four full collections to date, most recently *Over Misty Plains* (Indigo Dreams, UK, 2012). For more information please visit AlessioZanelli.it

Zavlanov, Gleb is a young poet and songwriter living in New York City. He is a 2017 graduate of Townsend Harris High School.

Zawadzki, Jarek was born in 1977. He lives in Gliwice, Poland. In 2002, he graduated from the University of Warsaw with an M.A. degree in Chinese Studies, and in 2017 he was awarded an M.A. degree in English Studies by Jagiellonian University in Krakow. He works as an Asian Market Manager for a woodworking factory. He is also a freelance translator in a combination of three languages: Polish, English, and Chinese.

Zhu, Wandi is studying English language and literature at the University of British Columbia, and is a former professional dancer who performed with Shen Yun Performing Arts.

CPSIA information can be obtained
at www.ICGtesting.com
Printed in the USA
BVHW091911270221
601159BV00004B/113